Reviews

In the follow-up sequel to *Finding Heart Horse, A Memoir of Survival*, memoirist Claire Hitchon reveals the difficult home life that led to her self-destructive adolescent years on the streets of Toronto in the late '60s.

The Wall of Secrets is a painful example of adoptive parenting gone wrong and adoptee resilience in the face of abuse and neglect. Claire's adoptive mother believes Claire to be her own personal emotional punching bag and uses any opportunity to put her down, to remind her of her worthlessness. Quixotically, she keeps track of every single expense of raising Claire—as if to put a price tag on what her daughter should owe her "selfless" mother.

But Claire is strong. Claire is resilient. Claire raises her own daughter on her own, getting herself clean, educated, and finding a fulfilling career as a registered nurse.

Like many adoptees, it's not enough. She still yearns to know her first mother, to find out where she came from. And like most reunions, it is nothing if not emotionally wrenching and complicated. Throughout, we see Claire's evocative descriptions, her raw feelings, and her deep love for family and nature. I highly recommend both memoirs.

Laura Dennis
Adult Adoptee in Reunion
Author of *Adopted Reality: A Memoir*

A secret only holds power when it's held and protected. Through the healing process of writing, with complete vulnerability, love, and letting go, Claire tells hers beautifully.

Tammy Chater, Traditional Chinese Medicine RAc

Claire Hitchon, in her sequel to *Finding Heart Horse*, the new memoir *The Wall of Secrets,* faces many of the painful memories and the possibilities that didn't become realities. She transitions from being "an invisible child" and feeling like no-one's daughter, with a "borrowed life," to the discovery of her true self and a life in which she "finds the diamonds" and discovers the beauty of life and her present existence.

Here is a beacon for us all: inspiration and encouragement to never give up on ourselves or on the life we might lead, if we become courageous enough to face the past, however painful and abusive, and move forward.

Von Coates
Adoption Blogger, Activist, and Post-Adoption Consultant

The Wall of Secrets

of

MEMOIR OF THE ALMOST DAUGHTER

CLAIRE HITCHON

*A secret only holds power when it's held and protected. Through
the healing process of writing, with complete vulnerability,
love, and letting go, Claire tells hers beautifully.*
—Tammy Chater, Traditional Chinese Medicine RAc

BALBOA
PRESS

A DIVISION OF HAY HOUSE

Balboa Press books may be ordered through booksellers or by contacting:

Balboa Press
A Division of Hay House
1663 Liberty Drive
Bloomington, IN 47403
www.balboapress.com
1 (877) 407-4847

Because of the dynamic nature of the Internet, any web addresses or
links contained in this book may have changed since publication and
may no longer be valid. The views expressed in this work are solely those
of the author and do not necessarily reflect the views of the publisher,
and the publisher hereby disclaims any responsibility for them.

The author of this book does not dispense medical advice or prescribe the use
of any technique as a form of treatment for physical, emotional, or medical
problems without the advice of a physician, either directly or indirectly. The
intent of the author is only to offer information of a general nature to help
you in your quest for emotional and spiritual well-being. In the event you use
any of the information in this book for yourself, which is your constitutional
right, the author and the publisher assume no responsibility for your actions.

Any people depicted in stock imagery provided by Thinkstock are models,
and such images are being used for illustrative purposes only.
Certain stock imagery © Thinkstock.

Printed in the United States of America.

ISBN: 978-1-4525-2393-4 (sc)
ISBN: 978-1-4525-2395-8 (hc)
ISBN: 978-1-4525-2394-1 (e)
Library of Congress Control Number: 2014921182

Balboa Press rev. date: 01/06/2015

For My Daughter

"In all of us, there is a hunger,
Marrow-deep,
To know our heritage,
To know who we are and where we have come from.
Without this enriching knowledge,
There is a hollow yearning.
No matter what our attainments in life,
There is still a vacuum, an emptiness,
And the most disquieting loneliness."

—Alex Haley

The Lotus Flower

The lotus flower symbolizes purity of mind or
divine creation of growth and knowledge.
From the muck of a pond and the murky water of samsara
(Pain, attachment, suffering) roots of the lotus reside.
With continued knowledge and growth,
A perfect bud emerges from the mud,
Gradually opening into an immaculate
white flower to rest on the surface.
It's an example of the harmonious unfolding of spirituality.
You yourself are the lotus.
You have the ability to grow out of the murky depths
And become the lotus flower in bloom, free
from worldly attachments and suffering.

Acknowledgments

This memoir was written, along with my first memoir, *Finding Heart Horse,* primarily as a transformative healing process. After eight years of rewrites, I realized I was no longer my story. It no longer defined me. My story was now in words between book covers. It was then I realized that my work was not over. With these books, I hope to challenge belief systems and give hope that lives can and do change.

I want to express my gratitude to the many teachers I've had, both formally and informally, and all those who helped me along the way.

Having a rare mast-cell disease has brought me many supportive friends, and along the way I met Janice Harper, who was so helpful in sorting out the hundreds of pages of stories and dividing them into two books. Thank you.

As I said previously in *Finding Heart Horse,* I am immensely grateful for the *Dakini* figures (female, energetic beings, spiritual muses, inspirational, wrathful figures in Tibetan Buddhism). Many have played a huge part in my growth as a person,

As the lotus, the one who emerged from the mud.

I am grateful to all the teachers of the Dharma that have passed through my life with many lessons to be learned, prayers to be spoken, and chants to be sung.

To my friends who have stood by me when I was in the depths of grief, pain, and illness, I will be forever grateful. Susan Wilson, Catherine Leigh, Darlene Smith, Karen Baker, Diane Richards, Joan

Carruthers, Bill Varela, and John Ostrander, thank you from my heart. A special thank you to Peggy Wildsmith for her friendship and care of my fur companion. My journey with mast cell disease is a difficult one. To know friends are available to jump in at a moment's notice while waiting for the ambulance makes these times bearable.

Tammy Chater, you are my lifeline and have been throughout this writing/life journey. I am so blessed to have you in my life.

To my daughter: I love you, always and forever.

Namasté.

Contents

Prologue

1957

When Mother is angry, she always puts her mouth in a straight line. Today, her lips will be straight lines all day. That's because it's Wednesday. Wednesday is piano-lesson day. Benny is Mother's first student and he always makes her mad. He's not good enough.

On Wednesdays, I hide in the library. It has a beautiful oak door that she always keeps closed. On the other side of the door is the only place in my world I feel safe. I know it's only a room, but it's magic. When I'm in there, I can think anything I want. I can pretend I'm just like the kids in the music room waiting for their lessons. They get to leave. I don't.

Mother's voice is getting louder. I know what that means. When she yells, my stomach always hurts. I wish Benny didn't have to come for his lesson first, because then she's mad for the whole day.

I'm in the hall. When I reach out to the left, I can touch the basement door. When I reach out to the right, I can touch the library door. I get nervous when I stand here. I'm not allowed behind either door by myself. I wish I were a ghost so I could just walk right through the door to the other side, but I'm not, so I can't. I have to go over the rules in my head about opening the door. It's important to know the rules.

It's also important to be quiet. That's a rule. It's not just her rule. It's my rule. I don't want Mother to hear.

"Benny! For heaven's sake, Benny, do it the proper way," she scolds. The loud crack of the pointer on the piano bench makes me jump. My heart goes faster and I hear pounding in my ears.

The rules, the rules, the rules, remember the rules.

It's two hundred steps from the library to the music room, but her voice goes right through the walls when she's angry. I hear Benny trying to play his scales. La, la, la, la, la. Over and over and over, up and down the ivory keys. I know them better than he does. I have to.

"Benny! Again, Benny, and this time do it right!" I can almost hear the line on her mouth stretching tighter.

I lean my face against the rough wood of the forbidden door. It feels like sandpaper on my cheek. The crystal doorknob jabs in my neck right where a necklace would rest, if I had one. But she says I don't need things like that; they'll make me vain. I don't know why she says that; she wears them all the time.

I peek through the keyhole, and there it is. The Wall. My Wall. It's inviting me to come in and look inside a drawer. I have to be careful. This door has its own story to tell. If I don't open it just right, it talks. It sticks in one place, close to the front edge, right at the bottom. It talks in a high-pitched squeak. It's such a tattletale.

Mother knows all of the house sounds, even from two hundred steps away. That makes me nervous.

"*Ben—nee,*" she screeches, "no sense doing anything if you don't do it right. Now do it again." Good. She's not listening to the door.

My face scrunches and my stomach rumbles. I know what's next: the loud crack of the pointer on the piano bench. Smack. Smack. Smack. He doesn't know how lucky he is. I always get the pointer on the top of my knuckles and it really, really hurts. She wouldn't do that to him or he would tell his mother.

My shoulders are all hunched up and stiff and my hands feel slippery, just like the fish my dad catches. I wrap my fingers around the crystal knob and move it half a turn. I lean my shoulder into the door, and it moves.

Benny is still trying to get his scales right. Good. That gives me more time to be in the library. With one leg in, I use my shoulder to push the door ever so slowly, until it's just wide enough for me to slip all the way through, into my secret world.

I'm in. I'm in. I'm in.

Simon says stop. So I do. Simon says listen. So I do. Simon says it's safe. So I move. I really like that game. I play it a lot.

Mother's voice is louder in here since the music room is one room closer. Benny is crying. She says all her students like her. I don't think Benny does.

I have to walk a certain way in here. I pretend I'm an airplane and hold my arms straight out. Then I have to balance on one foot, usually the left one. My right foot has to land on the fifth floorboard. Silence. I move my other foot up to match, and I wait. These floors have voices too, you know. Just like the doors. Certain places make certain sounds. If I step on the wrong one, she might hear me.

Step on a crack; break your mother's back.

I'm okay. I'm okay. I'm okay.

Ahead of me is the chair. That's where I'm going. I'm safe when its leather arms hold me.

A sudden chill in the air stops me in mid-step. Silence surrounds me like a wet blanket.

Did she hear me? What's happening?

I pretend I'm a statue and I'm holding my breath, staring straight ahead, waiting.

The bookcases stand in front of me with their shiny glass fronts. Today, twelve of me stare back. The faces looking at me have frowns. They look like those little soldiers in *The Nutcracker Ballet,* all dressed in red and black. Whatever I do, they do too. I know it's my reflection, but I like to pretend I have friends.

"Ben-nee. Can't you do better than that?" Her voice shatters the heavy silence. "Now, Benny. Now!"

My breath escapes with a whoosh. Mother is still in the music room. I didn't think she would leave Benny alone in there with all of her special things. I can't even go in there by myself, and I live here.

I gulp air like my guppy when he's on the top of the bowl. I swallow a dollop of air that's cool and smoky and tastes like last night's pipe flavor. Maple, I think. Good. I feel better now. I look back at the soldier girls in the glass fronts. I try to imitate what they do, arms at my sides, heels together. Mother always says, "No fiddling with your hands when you stand. Stay still. Put your shoulders back. Straighter."

The glass soldiers are wearing proper colors today. Her choice, not mine. Mother always says, "It's important to look neat and tidy. We want the other mommies to know what a good mother I am, don't we?" I don't think good mommies yell and hit their kids, but since she says I have to wear this, I do, for now, but not forever.

I have on stupid red leotards, too. The soldier girls in the glass have ugly pleated kilts on, blurry red, green, and blue. I really wanted to wear my blue jumper today, but the kilt was on my bed so I had to wear it.

I hate it. I hate it. I hate it. Someday, I'll wear what I want and never look like a soldier again.

Most days, mother does my hair in braids. She pulls so hard it makes me cry. I ask her to stop but she doesn't. She pulls so tight my face stretches.

"You have to be neat," she says, trapping the ends in elastic. When she isn't looking, I put my fingers inside the twists and wiggle them around to make them looser. Not messy, of course. She'd notice that. That would make her mad.

This morning she said, "If you don't smarten up, I'll chop this mess off, and then you won't complain." I don't know why she called it a mess. She fixed it. Later, she said I looked perfect. I'm confused. On the outside, I look perfect. On the inside, I'm messy.

"Pay attention to the notes, Benny." Mother's voice is really loud now. He's getting them wrong again. Over and over and over, Benny keeps getting it wrong. All wrong.

My eyes wander around the room. This room is special. Not like my room. In my room, there isn't much. I'm not allowed to have much, because that would just be clutter. My room's nothing like in here. In here, the colors are warm. There are old pictures, pretty lights, and interesting smells. And The Wall. It's not actually a wall—I mean, not like the walls of the room. It's a wall of drawers, hundreds of them. Mother says they are antique bankers' filing cabinets. She says it's not for using; it's just to be admired. She says I can't put anything in the drawers because I'd ruin them.

She doesn't know what I've put in those drawers. She never will. That's my secret.

I put my secrets in them. To me, the hundreds of drawers are just the right size for holding my secrets. The Wall is sort of magnetic. It wants me close. It wants me to open a drawer.

I can't, not yet. Not now, maybe someday.

Twenty steps ahead is Daddy's chair. Its chocolate-brown arms are reaching for me.

I'm coming. I'm coming. I'm coming.

Usually, I sit on the cold floor behind it so the corner can protect me. The chair guards the space between the door and the corner just for me. I told Daddy his chair had a face made out of buttons. He just laughed and said I was silly.

An island of wood sits in the middle of the room. Mother always says to use proper terms for things. To her, it's a desk. The corners are pointy-sharp if you bump into them. The wood looks soft and smooth, but it's not friendly like the leather chair. Besides, it's in the middle of the room, and that's not a safe place to be. I could step on the wrong place at any moment and then Mother would hear. It's best to stay where it's safe.

Behind the desk are two long windows with lacy curtains you can see through. The soldier girls don't show up in this glass, just the bookcases. If I want to see inside the cases, I have to look past the soldier girls.

Go away. Go away. Go away.

Each case has four layers filled with beautiful books full of stories I'm not allowed to read. Some have faded, gold letters and worn-out pages with strings of leather dangling from inside. I want to hold one in its leather coat and feel how heavy it is with words. I want to touch the writing inside with my fingertips. I want to trace the printing on the covers. Adventures wait inside. If only I could escape for a while.

I will someday.

Right behind the soldier girls' heads, on the fourth row, are the treasures. I really want to touch them, too. Shiny silver thimbles with tiny flower patterns tempt my finger to slip into them. There's a perfume-bottle collection in warm rose colors. I wonder if they still have perfume in them. Beside them, a garden of tiny china flowers grows: pink, yellow, and blue. I would never touch them. They're so delicate that they would crumble in my fingers.

Above the soldier girls' heads is the top of the case. Pictures stand there. Mostly of old ladies, dressed in long, faded skirts. Their hair is all twisted up on top of their heads. I wonder if I can put my braids up like that. I watch the soldier girls in the glass lift their braids up and pile them on their heads. Nope, that doesn't work. Braids drop and flop against my back.

One more look at the ladies. Daddy says they were his aunties. I love to look at their faces. Maybe, if I stare long enough and hard enough, I'll see something familiar. Mother says you need to love your family. I don't feel anything when I look at them. She doesn't feel anything but mad when she looks at me. Maybe we aren't really family.

My feet float silently across the wooden floor. I fall into the arms of Daddy's chair. A big, dusty cloud of air comes out. I breathe in Daddy's smells, a bit of musty air mixed with maple pipe and shaving cream. Leather arms wrap me in a warm hug. I snuggle in with my back against the old leather.

Is it safe to sit?

Just for a minute, just a minute. I'll be okay.

I neatly tuck in my red legs, and with my fingertips, I begin to memorize the fine cracks in the leather. The cracks look like broken glass. Daddy's grandfather sat in this chair. I wonder how late he got to stay up and read. I'd really like to sit here and read too.

A door slams. I hear a muffled conversation between two adults. That's Mother telling Benny's mom how his lesson went. She's always so nice to the adults. I'm not very worried about her finding me here, not yet, anyway. Her next student will already be waiting. I know because I've had lots of practice getting the time right to get out of here before she catches me. Too bad I can't tell Benny's mother about how my mother yells at Benny. But maybe even if I did, she wouldn't care.

My back fits right into the soft leather behind me. Around the cushion and along the arms and back are lots of buttons: small, round, leather buttons. Mother says it makes a chair valuable. I always count the buttons. First, I have to go over the rules. I made them up myself. Mother says that rules keep me out of trouble. I don't want to get into trouble.

My pointer finger circles the first button three times. Slowly. I have to really concentrate so I don't do it too many times. When I circle, I say, "I'm safe; I'm safe; I'm safe." That way, I stay out of trouble and I'm safe at the same time. It always works. I always feel better.

I use my middle finger on the next button. I circle it three times and say my verse. Then back to my pointer finger, and I start again.

I'm not allowed to count higher than a hundred. If it's longer than a hundred I might not be safe. Mother might come in and find me, and she would be so mad. That's why I need to count and say my verse.

Ninety- eight, ninety-nine, one hundred.

The leather is warm and soft as my fingers knead the worn, brown, leather puffs around my legs. The air smells of old people and old memories. I don't like my memories. They hurt me.

Time to go. I need to get to my safe place. My back softens and I uncurl my legs and slide over the edge of the cushion. As I melt into the leather slide the cushion makes, I glance around; it's not far to the corner. I counted three and a half steps. It's better to crawl. I'll pretend I'm a cougar, fast and quiet.

Pain shoots up my leg.

Ouch!

Things can be different from how they look. The floor looks warm and smooth, but it's not. Splinters with ends like Daddy's fish hooks wait to grab my knees. I slide my hand over the next few boards to make sure there aren't more. It's really cold. It's always cold. It looks warm, but in my house, everything is cold.

One more knee-step and I'm in my corner. There's enough space so that I can sit cross-legged, my back right in the corner. I'm safe in corners. If I lean over, I can see both sides of the library. I can't have more than one eye showing on the outside of the chair. That's my rule too. If Mother walked into the room and I leaned over too far, she would see me.

The corner walls are cold on my back. I don't care; at least I'm safe. One time, I heard Mother telling Daddy she wanted to change this room into a bedroom. That was horrible to hear. I couldn't stop worrying. This is the only place I have to be safe in. If I didn't have this room and The Wall, where would I put my secrets? Where would I be safe? Where would all the books live? I don't want to think about it too much. It makes me sad. Everything I like, she takes away.

I need to memorize everything in here in case she takes it away. My fingertips touch the cold floor under my legs. With both hands, I reach back to the walls on either side of me. I want to feel the wallpaper. It's a pretty design with a faded, green background. It's really the design I love to touch, not the paper. My fingers play over the edges, like I do when I practice the piano. *Five, four, three, two, one. Five, four, three, two, one. Five, four, three, two, one.*

When I get to the flowers, my fingers slow down. I think they used to be ivory lilies. I think they were shiny a long time ago. Not now. Now they're faded and dull, like an old garden. When I squint, I can see the flowers and leaves standing out from the faded, green-grass background.

I think the wallpaper is trying to escape too. Places along the edges are curling up. Sometimes, I help them. I pull them up, just a little. I'm glad nobody can see me do it. I would be in a lot of trouble.

Everything in here belongs together. The different woods, the leather chair, the pictures, the lights, and the books in their glass houses—it all belongs. Not like me—I don't feel like I belong anywhere. That's why I have The Wall.

Mother's voice has gone up an octave. I can see her in my mind: her lips pinched so tight, the words struggling to get out. "Janice, my goodness, Janice. Do I have to tell your mother about your scales? Play it again, and play it right." *Smack* goes the pointer on the piano edge, and the scale begins again.

I wiggle a bit to the right so I can see The Wall. I let my fingers circle the soft leather buttons on the back edge of the chair.

One, two, three. Four, five, six. Seven, eight, nine.

I'm safe. I'm safe. I'm safe.

Shivers of anticipation go up my arm. I always feel this way when I think about opening my secret drawer. My fingers squirm in delight. I begin to trace the front of drawer number twenty at the bottom left. Using my pointer finger as my pencil, I begin to sketch. There's a quarter-sized bald spot on the front where the varnish has worn off. The ridges feel like the wrinkles in old people's skin. The secret story in there is about the crumbs.

Last week, I was setting the dining room table for Mother's Church Ladies Group lunch. It was elegant, with sparkling glasses and soft, flickering candles bouncing light off the Silver Birch china. The starched white linens were crispy, just like she wanted. They're hard to iron. I burnt my fingers in two places.

I polished the silver until I could see my unsmiling face reflected back. I know where it goes. The glasses go here and the three forks there, and I know how to fold the napkin and place it across the plate.

I spent hours ironing, polishing, and placing so that everything was perfect. I thought it was pretty good for a kid of eight. "Can't you do anything right, you stupid girl?" she said. "How many times do I have to show you?" She snatched the napkin out of my hand and smacked me in the face with it. Then I had to re-iron it.

It's my job to do the kitchen work, prepare the table, play the piano when she asks, say the right words, and smile at the ladies. If I don't, I'm punished after they leave.

I thought using the Silver Birch dishes was funny. They didn't know that they weren't good enough to eat off of the Limoges dishes. Those were saved for more important people. Everything was placed exactly the same, each plate, each knife and fork—everything. Perfect, it all had to be perfect.

I stood at the door listening to old-lady church chatter. The clink of forks mixed with conversation about the Christmas concert and how wonderful Mother was to direct the children's choir again. Mother loves to hear these words. I want to gag and spit them out for her. The church ladies don't know the truth. They all live in pretend worlds. All wrapped up in themselves. They can't see beneath the Silver Birch, beneath the table, where I live in hell. Mother wouldn't believe I even know that word.

I stood at the doorway, straight, watching, anticipating everyone's needs. More water, more carrots in the bowl, more butter. And always Mother watching, waiting for a mistake.

Uh-oh.

There's a napkin on the carpet and crumbs too. I have to get that before she notices.

Quick. Quick. Quick.

Invisibly, I crawl under the table to grab the crispy linen now smeared with red lipstick and greasy crumbs. I know she's watching. I lick my fingers to pick up the resistant crumbs and put them into my hand. Mother moves her high-heeled foot closer to my hand, ready to jab.

Quick. Quick. Quick.

Instead of Mother's stiletto heel, I feel something graze over my head. A dry, thin-skinned hand like a chicken foot reaches down. The one with the beaded glasses chain is moving her chicken hand around until it finds the top of my head, my perfectly braided head. She pats me on the top of my head like a dog and then laughs like a hyena. I don't think it's funny at all.

I scramble out and have the napkin replaced with a new, perfectly ironed one and return to my post before anyone notices. Mother is watching. I'm waiting. I'm satisfied with the crumbs of affection I got under the table, for now, but not forever.

I close drawer number twenty tightly. I have so many secrets far worse than that.

At the bottom on the other side is drawer number forty-three. I call it "the happy drawer" because the label has an ink stain on it shaped like a smile. Out of the hundreds of drawers, this is the only happy one. It makes me sad to think about that. My heart has a hollow place that's dark and empty. A piece is missing and I don't know what it is. Warm, salty tears make little rivers down my cheeks. It stings a bit where I just bit my lip.

Don't cry. Don't cry. Don't cry.

My tongue curls up and snatches a tear. It reminds me of a frog catching a fly, and my lips curl in a smile.

I scrunch my eyes tight, squeezing the tear waves back inside their cave. I'm not allowed to cry. I'm not allowed to tell the secrets, so I have to put them somewhere for now, but not forever.

I focus on counting the buttons on the back of the chair. The Wall patiently waits for my return. It knows my routine. Sometimes I remember a special drawer, maybe one with very specific secrets, like the one at the very top on the left.

Drawer number five holds the secrets about the times Mother has hit me. One time, she chased me around the house swinging the heavy, ivory hand mirror that Grandma gave her. I don't remember what I did wrong, but she was mad. I was running around and she was swinging the mirror. It hit my face above my eye. My eyebrow came apart and blood spilled all over my clean dress; I knew that would make her madder, so I ran faster. She couldn't catch me.

The drawer at the right top, third down, drawer number seven, holds mean words. Mother says terrible things when she's angry, sometimes even when she's not. They hurt my feelings, but I don't say anything. She says I'm a child of Satan and that I don't belong here. She says I should be dead and she wants to get rid of me. Those words don't make any sense to me. How could I be a child of Satan when I'm her child? Does she think Daddy's Satan? I don't believe that. Daddy's nice to me. But he doesn't know my secrets.

Sometimes, when she's really mad, she says I'd better behave or she'll just send me back. Where does she want me to go back to? I don't understand, but I know my heart hurts. That drawer needs to stay shut.

I trace the drawers on the floor. When I dig my fingernail into the floor cracks, I pretend I'm opening one, just a crack, not really enough to look inside completely. I don't dare look all the way in right now, not yet. Someday, I will.

Some of the drawers are really sticky and hard to open, so I know I'll have to work really hard to get those open.

Mother's voice slides under the door, not quite as loud as when Benny was playing. Janice is a bit older and a bit better and doesn't get yelled at as often. She's trying to learn "Fur Elise." I can play that one with no mistakes. Tap, tap, tap; the pointer is keeping time with the metronome. Janice is behind.

The row of drawers that runs down the middle of The Wall is special. Those drawers hold surprises just for me, really good ones. There are beautiful dolls with long, honey-colored hair in curls, chocolate birthday cakes with candles, hair ribbons with sparkles, and smiling paper girls, the ones you get to dress up in paper clothes. I could call them present drawers—only, none of it is real. One of my friends from church has these things, only not in a secret drawer. They're in her room. I've seen them with my own eyes.

Sometimes, I wish so hard that when I squeeze my hands in a fist, it hurts. Then I press my eyes closed and say the words.

I wish. I wish with all my heart.

I wish they were real things in my room and not secrets in my drawers. Those drawers don't get opened very often either. They can only be used on very special days.

If I need to put a secret in one of the drawers, there are rules I follow. The more important or scary the secret is, the higher up The Wall it has to go. That's because it's harder to reach those drawers, and they are mostly the ones that are sticky anyway, like the drawer almost at the top corner.

Drawer number ten has the basement secrets. Those ones scare me at night. Mother yells a lot in that drawer. Like the time she said, "Get down there. Now. Move it." She gave my back a shove. I fell down the last few stairs and scraped my knees on the cement. I had to crawl inside the cold, dark root cellar. The door makes a grinding sound as it's shutting. It can't be opened from the inside. It's only a room for vegetables and fruits, not people. It has a gritty dirt floor and smells of over-ripe apples and budding potatoes mixed with rotten pears. Sometimes, I have to stay a long time in the dark. Sometimes, I get scared because there is a pipe that goes to the furnace room at the top corner and the rats walk along it to eat the fruit. I worry they'll eat me too. That's a really awful secret.

Bottom drawers have good things in them. I have a costume drawer. That's drawer number four in the middle. I can open it anytime and find a disguise to wear. I'm like one of those lizards that change colors depending on their surroundings—a chameleon, I think. This drawer has magic clothes. There's a long, sparkly fairy skirt with a magic wand that will change anything, anytime I want. There's a cowboy hat. It's a crispy vanilla ice cream straw hat with a tiny hole in the front and a red band. I'm going to wear it when

I catch my wild horse. There's a really big, black velvet cape with shiny red silk on the inside. It's so soft. Sometimes, I pretend I wrap myself up in it and disappear, just like that.

I know about these things because my cousin has them in her real costume box and one time, she let me play with them. Now, I have them in my drawer and I can use them anytime I want.

The air is thick and heavy. The silence is so loud my ears tingle. The library is dark now, the shadows almost gone. Only the golden light shines over the desk island. That means I have to leave. The table should be set and the potatoes cooking for dinner by now. Mother will be looking for me.

Get out quick. Get out quick. Get out quick.

I pull myself up from the corner, holding the back of the chair in one last hug. I quickly run my fingers over the buttons, wanting my time to be longer. One last look around, just to make sure nothing looks different, and then I have to leave.

It's always faster leaving. After spending time with The Wall, I'm a weightless spirit. I glide over the floor and magically appear on the other side. (Actually, it takes twenty-one steps to get to the door, but I don't count them. There's more magic when numbers are out of the picture.)

Heel to toe, right and left. Heel to toe, right and left. Heel to toe, right and left.

I slide through the space I left open and return to the house world. I pull the door shut being careful to not make any noise. I take two giant steps and I'm in the hall.

I'm out. I'm out. I'm out.

My feet move swiftly down the hall to the kitchen. As I turn the corner, I almost collide with Mother. She is standing with her hands on her hips, staring at the empty stove. She spins around as I come to a grinding halt. All I see are her thin, red lips. Her mouth is pinched and her lips are stretched thin, like two skinny worms. She forces out a grunt.

"And where were you? You know I like dinner started."

I don't answer.

Instead, I just grab the potato bag from under the sink. The corners of my own lips curl ever so slightly in what could become a smile. But I'm careful not to let her see. Already, I'm planning my return to the library and my Wall of Secrets.

Which drawer will I open tomorrow? What will I find? What will I have to put in?

Can't wait. Can't wait. Can't wait.

To myself I am only a child playing on the beach,
While vast oceans of truth lie undiscovered before me.
—Sir Isaac Newton

Chapter 1

On the Outside, Looking In

1977

The last time I saw my mother, she told me I was dead. "Dead to us," was how she put it as she leaned over my hospital bed, as I lay there with my wrists bandaged and bloody and my head hurting so bad it felt like someone had hammered nails into my brain. That was from all the pills.

"I'm so embarrassed," my mother wailed and then followed with a barrage of insults before she told me I could never come home.

Why would I ever want to go home? I wondered. I hadn't been home in years, not since I ran away when I was fifteen and ended up living on the streets of Toronto. Those were the wild years, the years of playing guitar, smoking pot, and running with Satan's Choice. They were a pretty rough motorcycle gang, but they were good to me. That's when I got addicted to heroin and things really got

1

weird. After I got out of prison, I started turning my life around. I couldn't have done it without my friend Daryl. She was an amazing woman and an amazing musician. We made such wonderful music together.

But then she got sick and died.

Shit happens.

I just couldn't handle any more shit in my life, so when she got really sick, I got the pills. I don't remember swallowing the whole bottle, and I sure don't remember cutting my wrists.

But I sure do remember waking up in the hospital to find my mother leaning over me, her red lipstick smeared across her mouth as thick as frosting, making her lips look like a gashing, blood-drenched wound, like the severed flesh of my arms.

"As far as we're concerned, you're dead to us," she hissed, then turned around, grabbed my dad by the arm, and walked out.

I first began to understand the terrible secret of my birth when I was eight years old. I didn't clearly understand it, but the truth started tickling my brain, like truth does sometimes.

I had this cousin who always let my cousins know they were adopted. They were two girls on my mom's side, and they'd been adopted and my cousin liked to point that out.

"You're not even real family!" she'd taunt them. "Your parents gave you away!"

I always bit my tongue when she said that. I didn't quite understand it completely, but I knew that they were real family and that my cousin was just being mean.

Then she started saying it to me.

That's when I knew just how mean she was, and that her words were just lies. She just said that about any cousin she didn't like, I decided. My other cousins, the adopted ones, said she was right, that I was adopted, too, just like they were. But I knew they were only saying that so they wouldn't feel so alone. Obviously, I wasn't adopted. I had baby pictures to prove it.

But that's when it started to tickle my brain.

What if I was?

So I asked my mom, a few times, but she just ignored the question or simply changed the subject.

She probably thought it was a ridiculous question.

Which it was.

When my mom said that I was dead to her, I thought about that cousin from my childhood. Maybe meanness runs in the family, I considered. But by that time, I was pretty used to it, so even though it hurt, I wasn't that surprised.

A couple of weeks later, I got discharged from the hospital and found a job.

It hadn't been easy finding work. I'd served two years in a minimum-security prison for possession of heroin, and while I was there, I finished my high school diploma and worked in various areas. That's where I learned many skills, but once I got out and tried to find work, the door always slammed shut the minute they asked me where I'd gotten my experience. It didn't matter that I'd been an honors student, an award-winning pianist by junior high, and was the only daughter of the Hitchons, one of Belleville's most-distinguished families. They just saw me as an ex-con, not worth $2.95 an hour. But this time, it was different. The man interviewing me didn't care about my past; in fact, he was intrigued.

He understood that creative people are imperfect and prone to rebellion.

He was quite a bit older than I was, by about twenty years. But he didn't seem old; he was one of those silver-haired, distinguished-looking guys who stay fit and are always well-mannered and beautifully dressed, a real "silver fox" if ever there was one.

I was so happy to just have work, especially since we were treated with respect. They never made me feel bad or out of place for having been in prison, and no one made a move on me. I kept waiting for it, at first, but pretty soon I concluded that all the guys, especially Mike, were just nice guys, real gentlemen. And he seemed to recognize that I didn't want to spend my life working in a minimum-wage job, but until I found something better, I was going to work hard and impress him, which he liked.

One day, after I'd just finished locking up and was getting my things together, I heard Mike call my name.

I turned around and he was standing there with a playful smile.

"How would you like to go get a drink and listen to some great jazz?" he asked, startling me with the question.

I sort of stammered in reply, and he just laughed and took the broken syllables that fell out of my mouth as a yes. So we went out and had a couple of glasses of wine and some dinner and then heard some jazz, and he took me home and didn't make a pass or anything; he was just the perfect gentleman. After all the motorcycle guys and the dealers and druggies I'd hung out with in the past, going out with a gentleman for a respectable drink and conversation made me feel really good, like I was a normal person.

We started talking a lot after that, about politics and religion, art and music. He seemed eager to talk, and I was eager to listen, since I hadn't had such interesting talks since Daryl had died. He took me to expensive restaurants and shows, and he was proud to be seen with me. I figured I was probably eye candy for him, but I felt so comfortable with him as I got to know him, and he clearly cared about me. So the age difference didn't mean much, and if he liked being seen with a pretty young girl every now and then, I felt lucky to be that girl.

For the longest time, there was nothing sexual about our relationship, but after some time, that changed. I hadn't felt that comfortable with a man in a long time, and for once, I felt genuinely cared for.

"I don't like you living here," he told me. "It's not safe living downtown, especially for you. There are too many temptations and bad influences, and you don't need that. You should move closer to the lake, someplace where there's nature, where you can meditate and heal."

I knew he was right; I have always felt most at home when I'm closest to nature, and it was true that I was tempted by the downtown crowd. I'd drop into my favorite places, The Continental and Norm's, every now and then, and I knew it was only a matter of time before I would end up right back in that life if I didn't do something to get away from it.

So Mike helped me to find a nice little apartment close to the water. It was a large studio with a big kitchen; it was clean and filled with light. I didn't have much to furnish it with, as I had been living with whatever junk I happened to find, but Mike built me some bookcases that divided the living area from the sleeping area, and I started to accumulate furnishings bit by bit. Before long, I went from having nothing to having an apartment filled with beautiful things. Mike would drop by with a bottle of wine and read me poetry or take me out to dinner, and life was very good.

But I was still pulled to the past, and I was unable to completely break free from it all. On days that I wasn't working, I'd scramble over the concrete to my favorite table at The Continental. The girls seemed to accept me in my new, respectable role, but every now and then, I'd catch them whispering back and forth, only to glance back at me with a phony smile. I knew what they were saying: that I thought I was better than they were, that I wouldn't make it in my new job and would be back to the street life in no time. That it was only a matter of time before I'd be back on heroin. They could say what they wanted behind my back, but it wouldn't change my determination. I wanted a better life, and I was going to do what I had to do to get it.

My life was slowly falling into place. Still, there was a persistent, haunting theme that enveloped me, smothered me in sadness and pain. And I didn't know how to break free. All I knew was that wherever I went, I didn't feel like I belonged. I wanted to find the place and people that were mine—my tribe. It wasn't at The Continental or Norm's, and it wasn't at work, but Mike seemed to understand that.

"Let me help you," he said. "Just trust me. All you have to do is trust me."

And little by little, I eventually did.

Being unwanted, unloved, uncared for, forgotten by everybody.
I think that is a much greater
Poverty than the person who has nothing to eat.
—Mother Teresa

Chapter 2

Broken Eggs

"Shit. What's wrong with me?" It was the third time I'd fallen asleep on the Queen Streetcar after work. Each time, I would end up at the last stop of the line and have to turn around and go back. It seemed that the hotter and muggier it got, the more tired I became, until by the end of my shift I'd come home from work so tired I couldn't even stay awake long enough to reach my bus stop.

"Maybe you should see a doctor?" the driver said as he turned to make the long drive back.

"Right," I replied, "maybe I should. I've been feeling pretty sick, too. I'll make an appointment." I closed my eyes and struggled to stay awake while I squeezed in as much rest as I could until we reached my stop.

When I finally got home, I didn't even bother with dinner; I just climbed straight into bed. I made a doctor's appointment the next morning.

"We can see you today," the receptionist told me. "Can you make it in this afternoon?" The thought of spending my day off riding the bus route yet again just to sit in a doctor's waiting room was not exactly fun, but I agreed to come in.

The next day, while I was working, the telephone rang. "Claire? It's for you!" the guy at the front hollered to me. I grabbed the extension and waited for the familiar click, to be sure he wasn't listening in. It was someone from the doctor's office calling with my test results.

I was pregnant.

I hadn't thought that I could get pregnant. I had been in the hospital several times for ovarian cysts and endometriosis. They told me I would never get pregnant. But for years, I'd very much wanted to have a baby, and in the back of my mind, I hoped and prayed that it would happen. Now that it had, I was in shock. Pregnancy was something that happened to other people, not to me. Having and raising a child was something that other people did, not me. Being unmarried and broke with a job that paid nothing was something that happened to other people, not to me.

This was happening to me.

I got through the rest of my shift in a daze as reality began to sink in. A million and one thoughts overtook my mind, but none seemed to settle long enough for me to focus on anything. It was all so surreal.

But it kept me awake long enough to reach my stop.

"No more sleeping?" the driver called as he pulled to the curb.

"Nope; not today," I said, as cheerfully as I could muster, before I stepped onto the curb and waved good-bye. As I walked home, I instinctively moved my hand to my still flat belly, as if to protect the rice-sized being from exposure the cruelty of the world.

I'll be okay. I'll be okay. We'll be okay.

As I walked and repeated my mantra, I realized that I had become a *we*. I had never really known what it was to be a *we*; it seemed that my entire life, I'd been alone.

I didn't really understand what *we* could mean, until it was taken away from me. I'd always assumed my family was a *we*. We liked to do certain things. We liked music. We were refined and important people.

But when I was ten or eleven, I overheard my grandmother and aunt having a conversation about me, and it shattered my sense of *we* forever.

They were talking in hushed tones, like a loud whisper, just soft enough for me to know they were talking about something important, but loud enough for me to hear them say it.

"She's doing so well," my aunt said to my grandma, "for an adopted child."

"Yes," my grandma agreed, "she fits in so well with the family, and it's so nice that she's musical like her parents."

I couldn't believe my grandma said that. Had she been talking to my cousin and listening to her mean lies? Why would my grandma say something like that?

I didn't quite understand it, but I did understand one part of it.

If I fit in so well, it must mean I was some kind of substitute. I wasn't a real part of *we*. They were a *we*, and I was a *she*. *She* fits in so well.

Now, grown and pregnant, I truly was a part of a *we*. When I opened the door to my apartment, everything looked different. The sudden realization that everything about my life was about to change gave me a new set of eyes to see my world. Where would I put a crib? Where would a child play? My little apartment, just right for me, had suddenly become too small.

I opened the fridge to grab a beer and then realized I shouldn't do that. I grabbed a carton of milk and laughed. It wasn't that long ago that I wouldn't have thought twice before reaching for heroin to shoot into my veins, and now with the realization I was having a baby, I wouldn't even reach for a beer! Why hadn't I protected myself in the same way I was already protecting my baby?

I plopped into the big, gray chair in my living room and set the glass of milk on the coffee table and thought.

Who should I call?

It seemed like I should call someone, tell someone the big news, but who? Who would really care if I was pregnant?

Mike, obviously, but I was too nervous to tell him. I had to live with my news a bit longer before it became "our news."

As I thought and thought about all the people in my life that would care, and how many of them had died or disappeared in the last few years, I realized how alone I really was. The silence of my apartment grew louder until the tears falling down my face were all I heard.

I wasn't crying because I was pregnant. I was crying because I couldn't think of anyone who would care.

The next day, I called in sick. No one asked what was wrong, so I called in sick the day after that, and the day after that. By the time I went back and realized no one had really even missed me, I felt even more alone. How had that happened? Everything had been going so well: my life was turning around, I was working, and I was seeing a wonderful man who treated me well. What happened?

What happened was that I'd suddenly realized how false all that joy had been. It was false because now I was suddenly in need of love and support, and now that I realized how much I needed it, I was terribly frightened of being alone. And the more frightened I was, the greater the walls were that I built around me, until I was all but certain no one cared, not even Mike.

It was easy enough to avoid him at first. He had so much going on and so many businesses to attend to that for the first week, I didn't even see him. And I was pleased about that, since I couldn't keep any food in my belly and was throwing up all the time. Then I found some blood in my pajamas and panicked. I called the doctor but he said to rest and not worry so much. That was easy for him to say. He didn't need to worry.

I did.

I had to learn real fast how to have and raise a child. How could I possibly do that when I still felt like a child myself?

So I decided to call my parents.

I hadn't spoken to them since my mother told me I was dead to them, and that had been a few years ago. My hands shook as I dialed the familiar number; I watched the rotary dial spin back into place and felt grateful that it slowed the whole process down. But as soon as I heard the phone start ringing, I felt all those years of anger and fear start boiling inside me. I wanted to scream at her for everything she'd done to me, scream at her for her cruel and heartless words when I was so sick and in the hospital, scream at her for going to my apartment and getting rid of everything I'd owned while I was hooked up to tubes. She'd just gone over to my apartment and cleared it out, as if she had the right to do so.

But I couldn't scream.

I needed her. I needed my mother, needed her to know that I was having a child of my own. I needed her to stop punishing me and just be my mother for once.

"Hello?"

I froze. Felt around in my throat for some words.

"Who is this?" Her voice hadn't changed at all. It was still the brittle, angry noise that I'd always heard come out of her mouth.

"Claire." My voice was barely audible. I cleared my throat and said it again. "It's Claire."

There was silence.

"I want to tell you something," I said, feeling a little bit stronger. After all, there was no reason to be scared. This time, I wasn't calling with bad news. This time, I was calling with great news; surely she'd be happy to hear she was going to be a grandma.

"I'm pregnant!" I blurted out. I didn't intend to say it quite that way, to make it the first sentence I uttered, but her silence had rattled me into just coming right out with it.

"What? What do you mean you're pregnant?" she said. "Why would you do that to us at this difficult time? My mother is dying. I don't want to talk to you about your problems. You have no business calling here." Then I heard the phone click, and a moment later, the dial tone. I slowly replaced the receiver onto its cradle and wiped away my tears with the sleeve of my blouse.

What had I expected? Did I think after all these years that she'd suddenly thaw and turn into a mother? Turn into *my* mother, to comfort my fears, share my joy, and give me motherly advice to help me become a mother myself?

The tickling truth finally sunk in when I was about twelve. My mother kept a big, old sugar tin in the pantry stuffed with important papers. It was a huge sugar tin for storing enough sugar to survive the Cold War, which made it all the more intriguing. I was told again and again that I wasn't to get into those papers, which naturally made me determined to do just that.

So one day, I waited for them to go to choir practice, and when I knew they were out of sight, I got into it. There was a stack of papers inside maybe two and a half feet high. I started going through them and at first, it was just a bunch of boring stuff, legal documents and things like that.

But then I got to something very curious and disturbing. It was a single sheet of paper. It was about a "birth mother," and it described a woman who was having a baby. It said that she was tall, attractive, musical, artistic, and loved horses. The paper was very official looking, and my parents had kept it in an envelope for some reason.

As I stood there holding that piece of paper, I realized it was true. I really had been adopted. I copied down all the qualities of my birth mother and put the papers back.

Night after night, I'd get that piece of paper out and imagine the woman it described. Tall and beautiful, musical and artistic and loved horses; *she* was the perfect mother. She was just like me, except for the beautiful part, of course. Why hadn't *she* raised me instead of my awful mother?

I dreamed about that beautiful woman riding horses, the woman who was really my mother. One day, I'd find her, and then I'd be safe. *She* would understand me.

I tried to ask my mother again about being adopted, but she changed the subject, like always. That's when I knew my real mother was supposed to be a secret. But that was okay. My other mother didn't have to know that I knew. That would be *my* secret.

As I stared down at the telephone, I realized I'd expected too much of my mother. Of all the many times she'd turned away from me, refused to help when I asked, even told me I was dead to her, somehow, this telephone conversation hit me the hardest. I finally knew in a way I'd never been able to fully accept before, that I really was all alone. That just when a child needed her mother the most, mine had hung up on me.

But I did have Mike. Mike had been there when everyone else turned away; Mike had taken care of me when I could barely take care of myself. Mike had asked nothing of me but to trust him. I don't know why I still hadn't told him I was pregnant. Maybe a small part of me was afraid of his response, afraid I would lose him, but as I sat there alone in my apartment, feeling so sorry for my motherless self and wanting so desperately to be loved, I slowly realized that there was one person above all others who cared about me, and that was Mike, my baby's father. I had to tell him. Then everything would be all right. All I had to do was trust him.

"You're what!" Mike said, so stunned you'd have thought I'd just told him I was an alien from outer space.

I didn't bother to repeat myself. I just poured him another beer and waited for the news to sink in.

"I thought you said you couldn't get pregnant," he declared, clearly upset.

"That's what I thought, but apparently, I was wrong." I knew he wouldn't believe it, but that was the truth. I really did think I couldn't get pregnant because I'd been told by doctors that I'd had endometriosis that had left me with scar tissue and I probably couldn't get pregnant. I believed the doctors.

"All right," he said as he calmed down, "we'll take care of it." I began to relax, to allow myself to fall into the comfort he always provided. He would take care of me after all.

"But these things cost money, and we have to be discreet."

"What?" I asked him, confused by why and how he expected me to be "discreet" about a pregnancy. Why did I have to be discreet?

"Well, you aren't planning on keeping it, are you?" He seemed genuinely incredulous at the concept.

"Of course, I'm going to keep my baby," I told him. "I know what it's like to be adopted! I'm not throwing my baby away!"

"I wasn't talking about putting it up for adoption," he said, and I exhaled in relief. "I was talking about getting an abortion. I know a doctor—"

But I cut him off. I would never consider an abortion, even though in Canada, they were legal. I wanted my baby.

I took a deep breath, then looked him straight in the eye and spoke firmly. "I'm not having an abortion. I'm going to have a baby."

"Are you out of your mind?" he said, his voice rising. "You aren't ready to be a mother. You barely make enough to support yourself, and if it wasn't for me, you wouldn't even have this apartment!"

I couldn't believe what I was hearing. After all our conversations, all the laughs and whispers that we'd shared, all the assurances that I could—and should—trust him, now he was throwing my apartment in my face? All he did was help me find it and give me some furniture; I paid the rent each month, and I paid for my own groceries. I supported myself. But before I could even respond, he began listing all the things that were wrong with me and proved I was unfit to bear his child: I was a recovering junkie. I'd had hepatitis. I had no family to help me.

"And just what do you think being pregnant is going to do to your body?" he said. "Having a baby is going to ruin your figure!"

I was thunderstruck. I couldn't believe what he was saying.

But I knew what I was hearing: another dial tone.

A name is the first story that attaches itself to a life.
—Michele Kresler

Chapter 3

Tashi Delek

I sat in my big, gray chair and watched my belly rolling as if there were tidal waves inside me. Spasms of pain shot through me and I gasped for air.

"One and two and three," Jan counted, tracking the waves of pain that were coming closer and closer. I'd met Jan shortly after leaving work, and we quickly became friends. After a couple of months, she moved in with me to help out, and now she was by my side, holding my hand as I squeezed so tight I was afraid I'd break her fingers.

The last six months had been hard; they'd been life changing, in fact. But they'd prepared me well for safeguarding the life I was about to give to the world. There was no way I would ever give this baby away; I couldn't imagine giving away the child I'd cradled in my womb for nine and a half months, the child who was two weeks late and taking all the time in the world to arrive while my body slowly split apart in agonizing pain. The child that responded to certain music I would play on the piano and kicked like crazy when I had to have dental work done. The child that settled when I spoke softly to her and massaged my belly. Babies know these things. They learn in the womb and feel the energy of positive and negative connections with their mother. I read that; I believed it, and she proved it.

Pregnancy had changed me. It had forced me to realize my life had a purpose. I spent every minute reading the best books I could find on pregnancy, prenatal care, and babies. I exercised daily and watched what I ate. I ate only the right food groups and supplemented my diet with the best vitamins. I played the piano to let the music soothe the kicking feet that protruded from my sides at different times of the day. I felt healthier than I had ever been, and I noticed a glow in my skin and a sparkle in my eyes that I hadn't felt since I was in the Rocky Mountains hanging out with the wild horses. And whenever I felt overwhelmed, I let my mind wander back to those mountains and imagine, in my mind's eyes, my favorite horse, the one that I'd named Dali. It took only a moment of meditating on those moments of the past for me to feel relaxed and rejuvenated and prepared for whatever was to come.

Finally, as it was nearing midnight, we made the trip to the hospital. They wouldn't let Jan come in with me, so I was left alone with a group of Italian and Portuguese women who spoke little English. None of us were in the mood to chat; the screams erupting from their mouths were terrifying, and it wasn't long before I was screaming right alongside them. We sounded like torture victims pleading for mercy as the sweat poured down our faces and we panted and cursed, all night long.

By 9:00 a.m. the next morning, Good Friday, I welcomed my daughter into the world.

"Give her; give her to me; give her," I insisted as I motioned to the nurses to hand me my baby as fast as they could.

My newborn girl was placed onto my chest, her eyes wide and bright. When our eyes locked, it was magic, a moment that will be etched in my mind forever. I wrapped my arms around her little body and gazed in wonder at how tiny she was. I moved my hands over her body, made sure she had all her limbs, all her fingers and toes. I brushed my hand across her little face, touched her nose and her perfect little lips, and whispered her name, to her. In Tibetan Buddhism, which I had been practicing and studying for some time at that point in my life, *Tashi* means "auspicious." Often used in a greeting of respect, *Tashi Delek* means, "May all auspicious signs come to this environment;" or, "Blessings." I wanted the world for my little girl, all of the goodness that life can bring.

Suddenly, she began to cry and suck for air, her cries so loud they alarmed me. I pressed my lips into the soft fuzz of her hair to calm her and told her in the softest voice, "Welcome, little one. You are perfection."

I couldn't stop staring at her. For the first time in my life, I had a genetic connection to someone; for the first time in my life, I was related to someone. My daughter.

A pair of sterile gloves reached out for her, and I followed the latex hands up a pair of arms to the face of another nurse, who came to take my baby away. My arms tightened around her, the primal need for a mother to safeguard her baby pouring from every cell in my body. The smell, the touch, the sound of her softening cries, all were hardwired into my soul, and this woman wanted to take my little baby away! I just couldn't imagine how any mother could let her child go.

Why had my real mother let me go? Why did she give me to such a horrible woman? Was there something wrong with me?

The nurse gently pried my arms from my baby and expertly scooped her into her arms and took her across the room to be weighed.

"She's just beautiful. Weighs in at seven pounds even," the nurse said.

I tried to push myself up so I could see her, but I was all tied up in tubing like a trussed turkey.

"You'll see her later, dear. Lay down now and get some rest," another nurse said as she pushed me back onto the bed. "She's just going to the nursery now; we'll bring her back soon, I promise."

As I watched them wheel the incubator out the door with my precious daughter, I fought the urge to roar like a mother lion. I wanted to scream, "Bring her back! That's my child! Give her back to me!" But the words were stuck in my throat, just waiting to burst forth.

Had my own mother ever wanted me brought back? I wondered. Tears began to flow down my face, an emotional flood of overwhelming joy and deep, eternal pain. When I looked into my daughter's eyes, I realized I was also looking through my own birth mother's eyes, and I felt her own pain and grief. The pain now belonged to us both, birth mother and lost daughter. We'd been connected in body and spirit for nine months; we shared blood, nourishment, and life itself. Severing that primal connection shattered two people's psyches, extended the pain of birth across our lives. What purpose could such a disconnection serve? How could it be possibly right?

I could not understand my own questions, much less the answers, so I put my thoughts into my Wall of Secrets so that I could focus on the miracle that had come into my life. A newborn child had been given to me to care for and love, and that meant more to me than any loss I'd ever suffered.

When the nurse brought her back to me, I held her to my breast and watched her suckle her mother's milk. She was so peaceful, so content, and so perfect.

Anxious, the bird lost from its own flock
The sun sets and still it flies alone,
Back and forth with no place to rest,
As night wears on, its cry grows sadder.
—T'Ao Ch'ien

Chapter 4

Crossroads

Should I call her? Will she hang up again? Does she even care?

I wanted to call my mother. I wanted to tell her about my new little baby girl, let her know she'd become a grandma. But I knew if I did, she'd probably just hang up again. So why did I? Why did I pick up that phone and dial her number?

Because I couldn't imagine anyone turning her back on this precious baby—her own grandchild. It seemed wrong to not let her know, to not give my daughter a chance to have a family, a real family, however damaged it might be.

I hesitated before lifting the phone off its cradle. The receiver felt like a fifty-pound barbell as I struggled to bring it to my ear. My fingers dialed the number automatically, my brain not even thinking of the numbers that had been etched in my mind since childhood.

"Hello?" My mother's dramatic voice penetrated my ear.

I thought of hanging up, slamming the phone back down, when she asked, "Who is this?"

"It's me," I replied in a whisper. "I had a girl. I thought you would want to know."

There was a moment of silence, a sliver of a second when I thought I could hear her heart melting, before she said, "That's nice, dear, but I have company at the moment. Good-bye." And then I heard the click of the phone and the line went dead.

The receiver slipped out of my hand. I fumbled to pick it up and placed it back on the cradle. Then I took some deep breaths and made another call, to Mike.

"I just wanted you to know you have a daughter," I told him, trying to be as pleasant as possible. "I remember you said you'd always wanted a girl."

"That's nice," he replied. Then he added, "Don't call here again."

I slipped under the covers, buried my head in the pillow, and closed my eyes to block out the world. Why didn't anyone care?

The next day, a nurse came into my room. She wasn't one of the familiar nurses; the moment she entered, I knew something about her was different. Her smile, it seemed too phony, like she was about to sell me a diaper service. She clearly wasn't coming into the room to take my pulse; that was for sure.

"How are you today, Miss Hitchon?" she asked in a honey-soaked voice.

"I'm fine," I said. "What do you want?"

Her fake smile got bigger and faker. "I just wanted to introduce myself and see if I could be of any help to you. I'm a public-health nurse and I work with unwed mothers to help them make decisions about what's best for their babies."

The world stopped. Froze. Everything fell silent.

"You mean you are here *to try to take my baby away?*" I said, my voice rising with each syllable.

"Now, now," she said in a voice so patronizing that I wanted to throttle her. "I just wanted to tell you about some of the childless families we have who want to give a home to a beautiful, healthy baby like yours."

"Get out!" I shouted, so loud I shattered her face with my words. She looked like I'd just slapped her.

"Miss Hitchon, I know you love your baby and wants what's best for her and—"

"Get out!" I shouted again, growing furious.

"But she would make such a beautiful gift to a young family—"

Just as I was about to throw my bedpan at her, two nurses, summoned by my shouts, rushed into the room and asked what was going on.

"This woman wants to give my baby away!" I said, pointing at her.

"But, but—" she stammered, but that was the end of her.

They kindly escorted her out.

Several other public-health nurses came by over the next few days, and each time, they received the same response from me. It was incomprehensible to me that they would just assume that because I wasn't married, I would give my baby to someone else. Sometimes they just hung around and watched me bathe her; feed her, change her diapers. They were like vultures waiting, and rather than continuing to battle them, I did my best to stay calm and polite. There was absolutely no way they were getting a hold of my baby, so if they wanted to watch me wipe up her poop, then let them. All I wanted to do was go home where I could hold my baby to my chest and stare at her as long as I wanted.

If it had been up to me, she would have been with me constantly, but like many newborns; she was jaundiced and needed treatment under the hospital's bilirubin lights. I would stand for hours and watch through the glass. It reminded me of when my own skin was yellow and I nearly died from hepatitis. I couldn't bear the thought that she could die.

"It's completely normal," a nurse assured me. "It has nothing to do with your hepatitis. Newborns are born all the time with a touch of jaundice. It's because their livers are still developing, but she'll be fine; you'll see."

Still, I worried. Nothing the nurses or doctors could say would relieve my fears. I knew how close to death I had come and worried myself sick over the possibility that she didn't just have something newborns get all the time. Our blood types were both RH negative, and that could cause problems. How did they know she hadn't picked up something from me, that some of my hepatitis wasn't hiding away in my own liver? How did they know?

My tears began to drip from places hidden away deep inside me, leaving wet patches on my blue hospital gown. No one could understand why I was so worried, but I knew. I knew how easily my child could be taken from me, if not by the public-health nurses, perhaps by God. I wasn't even religious, but I prayed my new baby would be all right.

Over the next few days, I watched the faces and babies change, new mothers wheeled away to be discharged, their laps piled high with flowers and gifts. I had no piles of baby clothes or flowers on my night table, though work sent a gift—I don't even remember what it was. Everyone at work signed it. Nobody from work came by. I didn't have many visitors at all. But I didn't really care about that. I knew I had the best gift of all, and she was all I wanted to bring home.

When we were finally discharged, the snow was falling in large, fluffy flakes, blanketing us in their purity as we climbed into a taxi and went home. I carried her into my apartment, and for the next several days, I couldn't take my eyes off her. I traced each tiny wrinkle and memorized her pink tulip lips as I watched for her first smile. My thoughts were wild with plans for our future. My life's purpose lay wrapped in her pink, fuzzy blanket, snug and warm beside me. My love for her came from a place so deep, I was unaware it even existed. I never knew I could love anyone so much.

But loving my little girl touched a tender spot on my heart that made me wince. At times, the dark place that longed for my own mother—not the one who adopted and treated me with such hatred, but the one who bore and forsook me—brought pain and more tears. When that happened, I focused on my little daughter, and I put my pain in a drawer of The Wall.

Your vision will become clear only when you
can look into your own heart.
Who looks outside dreams; who looks inside awakes.
—Carl Jung

Chapter 5

Escaping into Reality

My sweet girl was six months old, and I still didn't have a job. I'd stare into her hazel eyes and rock her, knowing her future was in my hands, but having no idea how I'd give her that future. I needed to find work.

Every day, I poured through the classified ads and hoped to find something, but it seemed like there wasn't anything I was qualified for that paid more than minimum wage, and that wouldn't be enough to cover daycare. I needed a good-paying job, a professional job. It seemed there were lots of ads for teachers and nurses, but I only had a high school diploma. My eyes kept roaming toward the nursing ads. When my friend Daryl was dying, I'd spent so much time in the hospital with her that after awhile I started taking classes to be a lab technician, but I hadn't finished those. When Daryl died, so did a piece of my heart. Would any nursing program even take me?

I still had those old lab-tech books, and I remembered how much I enjoyed slipping on a lab coat when I was visiting Daryl, sneaking among the hospital staff as if I was one of them, and accompanying her when she went for her tests. We got a kick out of that, Daryl and I, and I still found myself laughing at the private joke she and I shared. I had felt so happy helping her.

Could I? Should I? Was it even possible?

I got out the phone book, looked up nursing schools, and found a number. I picked up the phone and started to dial; I hoped that my daughter wouldn't wake from her nap and I'd have to hang up before I got my answer.

A woman answered the phone. "Hello? May I help you?" she asked.

"Hi. I'm interested in registering. Can you tell me: If a person has an arrest record, would she still be able to be a nurse?" My heart thumped against my chest as I waited for her answer.

After a long pause, her words shot from the phone like frozen darts. "No. Of course not; we have standards, you know. Do you have any other questions?"

"No. I believe you told me what I need to know," I answered. "Thank you."

I hung up the phone and knew right then and there that I was going to prove her wrong. I was going to become a nurse, come hell or high water.

A year and a half later, I proudly walked across the stage to receive my Registered Nursing Assistant's diploma. I'd graduated with first-class honors and was encouraged to continue with my nursing education.

I began my professional career in a hospital in the downtown core. Only a few short years before, I had been among the most damaged of that downtown core; I was addicted to heroin, sick and

malnourished, and I'd wake up to find dead bodies in my bed—
when I even had a bed. Sometimes I even slept outdoors because
I had no place else to go. Now I was caring for some of the same
people I once knew—or at least, people very much like them.

The deaths of friends and the life of my daughter had turned
my own life around and helped me to realize how short life is and
how precious. Now I had a profound responsibility to assure that my
daughter had the best life possible. Each day, as I put on the crisp,
white uniform and cap that marked me as a nurse, I wanted to pinch
myself to make sure it wasn't a dream. My child had given me the
gift of not just her own life, but of mine. She'd made my dreams of
motherhood, family, and a nursing career come true.

I continued to practice and study Buddhism, a philosophy
that helped me to cope with the uncertainties and pains of life. I
discovered that the power of a spiritual life would save me again
and again from disappearing into nothingness. I began meditating
and rethinking my past assumptions to discover that nothing is
permanent; everything changes. For so long, I had clung to my
identity as an addict and an invaluable street kid. Shaking off the
past was hard, but through Buddhism, I began to see that I did not
have to remain in the past, and I did not have to cling to an identity
that no longer fit me. I was growing, just like my little baby, who one
moment was crawling on her little belly like a plump little fish out
of water and the next was rising up on her feet to tackle the world.
We were growing together, changing daily.

After a few months of working for the hospital, I switched to an
agency that would send me out on different assignments around the
city. Agency work allowed me to work in a variety of positions, so
that I could have a better idea of what I would eventually specialize
in, and it gave me more control over my time. If my daughter was
sick, I didn't have to worry about who would watch her; I could just

stay home. And if I needed a break or just wanted to spend more time with my little girl, I didn't have to ask anyone for time off, I just took it.

On those days, the two of us would go to the parks, to the beaches, or just shopping. What a joy it was to share the little things and see the world through her eyes, which were so filled with wonder and curiosity. She loved the colorful shops, the music in the streets, the beautiful parks, but for me, the area held a different meaning.

These were the streets where I'd lived a different life, the life of addiction and rebellion. As I remembered that life, I felt a peculiar mix of darkness and happiness. I had memories of bad decisions and terrible consequences alongside memories of wild times and wilder friends—memories that weren't entirely bad at all; for all the pain they'd brought me, they had also provided me a place where I belonged, where I fit in, a place where I had friends. And every once in awhile, we'd run into some of these friends, and shivers of recognition would creep under my skin as we embraced and caught up in conversation. I felt familiar among them; after all, I'd grown up with these women. I knew they cared about me and they understood my need to have a different life, especially Shelly.

Shelly was a tough one, a real downtown legend. She was half Asian and half mean. Nobody messed with Shelly. We met when I was sixteen and she nearly thirty. She hung out with the Continental Bar crowd, as I did, but she'd been around a long time before I came along. Yet for all her hard living and tough talk, I could tell from the moment I met her that she had a tender heart buried under that rough exterior. I felt an instant connection with her, but it took many years before we really got to know each other.

It wasn't until we both found ourselves locked up together in a minimum-security prison on drug charges that we really became close. Shelly was trying to get her life straight. Being locked up helped us both to get off drugs, and we spent many hours sharing our dreams of cleaning up our lives and making something of them.

Shelly had looked out for me in prison, and since I'd been in Vanier awhile by the time she came along, I looked out for her. After we got out, we kept in touch every now and then. Shelly's two daughters were living with her brother. But once she was off drugs and back on her feet, she wanted them back.

"I think we can make a good home for our girls," she said one afternoon after I had run into her. "We've been through so much together that we get each other like no one else will. And we both want good lives for our kids. Why don't we get a place?"

The thought was appealing, especially since my apartment was proving too small now that my growing girl was walking. Jan and I had parted ways just before my little girl turned two. A part of me was afraid that if Shelly and I lived together, we might both end up back on drugs. But a bigger part of me had greater confidence than that. All that mattered to me was my daughter and my work, and I wasn't about to forsake them. Together, Shelly and I could be mutually supportive.

"Give me some time," I told her. "I really need to think about this."

"Sure," she said, her hearty laugh assuring me that she, too, was confident it could work out. "When you're ready, just give me a call."

"Yeah, sure, I'll do that," I said and gave her a big, warm hug before we moved on.

"What do you think, Sweetie?" I asked. "Should we get a new place with Shelly? Would you like some big girls to play with?" She didn't understand what I was saying, but she was happy to hear her name. She reached up her little hands for me to pick her up and hold her close, and I did, holding her tight while she played with my large, bumpy nose. *Where'd that nose ever come from?* I wondered, thankful that she didn't bear it. It sure wasn't a Hitchon nose. Mind you, it had been broken many times. It was the nose my birth mother must have given me. *Did she have the same nose?* I wondered. A tear trickled down my face, and my sweet girl suddenly looked sad. We were connected in body and spirit; she could sense the slightest change in my emotions. I couldn't let her see me get sad. A big, happy smile opened across my face, and I tickled her little ribs until we were both giggling with joy. Yes, a family with other children, that's what my little girl needed. Maybe moving in with Shelly wasn't such a bad idea after all. Maybe it was just what we all needed.

It was right about that time that we were on our way home at the end of a busy day. I was looking forward to some deep contemplation at home, and then we passed a little kiddie's circus in a store parking lot. My little girl began squealing in delight the moment she heard the blaring sounds of musical rides and vendors hawking their food and wares and games. As we pulled closer, she saw the colors and clowns and lights and clapped her little hands together in excitement. Such a world was absolutely magical to a little girl.

"Okay, okay," I said, laughing despite my tired bones and weary spirit. "Let's go!"

"Pony, pony," she said, pointing to a pony ring where several small horses were tied.

We stood at the gate and watched the horses parade listlessly around with giggling children on their backs, when I was suddenly taken aback and gasped for air. A horse passed right in front of us whose markings were identical to those of a wild horse I had once watched from afar in the Rockies.

I had never forgotten that mountain adventure when I had trekked into the wild and waited for the chance to see some wild horses. When they finally arrived one early dawn, a mare that stood guard over her children mesmerized me. She was white with melting splotches of brown, and I named her Dali because she reminded me

THE WALL OF SECRETS

of Salvador Dali's style of paintings. And now, here she was again, only a miniature version of my majestic friend, her chocolate patches identical. Another interesting Dali theme played out in the art of my daughter's father and now again in this pony. My eyes were glued to her as she slowly put one foot in front of the other, her head hanging low in resignation to her fate in captivity. As she swung her head in our direction, I tried to catch her eyes, to lock them with my own just as Dali had a few years and a lifetime before.

I tightened my grip on her little hand and pulled her into the ring. "I have to see that horse," I yelled at the vendor and pointed to the mini-Dali. "That one. The one with the brown patches!"

"Calm down, lady!" he shouted back, irritated by my bossy behavior. "Wait your turn."

"Mommy, I want ride!" She pleaded, puzzled by my sudden change in mood.

"Wait, not now. Mommy needs to see something," I said, determined to get closer to the chocolate-splattered pony.

When the pony neared, I grabbed her weathered halter and pulled her head toward mine. Our eyes locked. But of course, it wasn't Dali. That would not have been possible. This was just a pony. What had I expected? Did I think that somehow my wild horse from years before had been captured and turned into a pony for a children's carnival ride?

My eyes brimmed with tears as I loosened my grip on her bridle and stroked her nose. Old memories from the past returned with a rush. How desperately I'd wanted to reach out and touch Dali, to run wild and free alongside her, but it was not to be. She had galloped away with her family into the wilds of the mountains, free and untamable. How desperately I'd wanted to belong to her, to belong to a family, to be free myself from the isolation of the human world.

"Mommy, mommy sad, mommy cry," my little one said, getting scared.

"Cripes, lady, move outta the way," the circus man yelled as he grabbed the bridle out of my hands. "Go on! Get outta here!"

I grabbed her hand and pulled her, screaming, out of the ring. She wanted to ride the pony so badly, but I had to get away. I just couldn't bear to look at that pony another second. It reminded me of something I'd found and lost. I couldn't bring myself to remember the wild horses; I was suddenly filled with an overpowering anxiety as I realized this pony was not my long-lost Dali. I had no idea why I was so consumed by my anxiety. What was I afraid of? I wasn't at all afraid of horses; I absolutely loved them. But the thought of losing my connection to Dali and her wild family somehow crushed me in an inexplicable way. I couldn't stay another moment.

"Later," I said. "Later, you can go for a ride, not now. Come on."

I pulled her along as fast as her little feet could travel as she cried and screamed for the ponies, until I spotted an ice cream stand.

"Let's get some ice cream!" I said, and at that thought, she started to smile. Ice cream is a mother's best friend in times like these.

With a cone in each hand, we sat and watched the circus spinning and sparkling about us. I looked over at her and started to laugh—she had so much chocolate smeared all over her face that she, too, looked a lot like Dali.

It'll never go away. I'll always be looking, searching, wanting to belong somewhere. Why can't I just settle for what is? Why can't I just accept that my own family didn't want me? Why can't I just accept that this sweet little girl is all the family I'll ever need?

She looked up as if she knew what I was thinking and offered me a bite of her ice cream cone. I laughed on the outside, but inside, I felt only sadness. I wanted to fully experience the daily joys like this moment, to embrace each perfect moment and accept it just as it is, as Buddhism teaches. But I knew from the past that whenever I became comfortable and allowed myself to feel joy, the hidden pain would appear just around the corner.

As we headed back toward the subway, I watched the sun disappearing into the background, the sunset erased by a curtain of smog. Here, in the middle of the city, covered in grit and grime, I felt as if my spirit was broken. Just when my life was beginning to turn around, just when everything was promising and exciting and filled with possibility, a moment of darkness would hit me hard in the gut, a flash of a memory like a flickering light about to burn out. I knew that the city would devour me—that I could never thrive in an urban environment. Like a wild stallion, I needed the wilderness and the earth's energy if I was ever to grow. But the wilderness was very far away. Would I ever have the chance to return?

The next day, I had my answer.

We do not create our destiny; we participate in its unfolding.
Synchronicity works as a catalyst toward
the working out of that destiny.
—David Richo

Chapter 6

There are No Coincidences

"So when are we going to get to meet that little girl of yours?" It was my friends, Paul and Joyce, who'd called me out of the blue. I didn't know Joyce well, but Paul was an old friend from the Yorkville days. A few years back, they had moved to Calgary so he could get work in the oil industry. Apparently that didn't pan out, but it sounded like they were doing all right nonetheless.

"You know we've got plenty of room here," Paul said. "Why don't you come on out for awhile and get some fresh air?"

Maybe it was a coincidence, or maybe something else entirely, but I couldn't help but think that receiving a call to return to the Rocky Mountains the very day after I'd had such a powerful memory of the last time I'd been to there was a sign that I needed to go.

"Let me give it some thought, and maybe we can make it out next month."

I spent the next few weeks on pins and needles, thrilled to think of actually returning to the mountains and filled with apprehension that if I did, I might not see the horses that I'd felt so connected with, which would somehow spoil the magic of a place that held such a treasured spot in my heart. There was also a horse of a different color haunting me, and that was Street Horse—heroin. Paul was a friend from the past, from the days of hard drugs and harder living, and as much as I treasured his friendship, I didn't want to trigger any desires to return the life I'd lived when we first met.

But I knew I had to go.

I found a cheap flight and flew to Calgary with an open-ended ticket. I wasn't sure how long we were going to stay, but since I had no idea when I could ever return to the mountains again, I wanted to spend some time there.

Paul met us at the airport, and after all the hugs and mutual admiration, we piled into his car and drove to their place, a small, brick bungalow not far from downtown. The house was rather shabby and jam-packed with people. Paul's brother lived downstairs, and the family lived upstairs. Joyce had three girls from a prior marriage, ages six, eight, and ten, and they were all gorgeous blondes. She also looked after a couple of other little kids. Money was tight for them, it was plain to see, and they were just scraping by.

"Your daughter can sleep with the girls in their room, and you can take the couch," Joyce said as she picked up toys as she walked across the room to show me where I'd be sleeping. "It's not much, but there's always room for one more!"

Having slept on park benches and in prison cells at various times in my life, I could easily handle a couch. We settled in for our visit, but we hadn't been there long before it was clear that Paul may have gotten off hard drugs, but he was far from straight and sober. I don't know what happened to his plans to get work in the oil fields, but from what I could tell, he didn't have much motivation to do anything. He spent most of the day at his brother's apartment downstairs, drinking and smoking pot while Joyce took care of the kids and the house. I pitched in with the housework and bought the groceries, and I paid them some rent money to help out. When my own money started to dwindle and it was clear Paul wasn't doing much to find work, I got out the classified ads and quickly found some work with the Red Cross collecting blood in the little oil-rig towns that surrounded Calgary. It wasn't ideal, but it paid enough to help out, and I could even save a bit for myself. And when I got home from work, worn out from being on my feet or driving around Alberta all day long, I'd often wander downstairs and join the guys for some beer and conversation.

It was a busy house, with lots of people dropping by. Paul had lots of friends who would come by with a six-pack or some weed, and while it wasn't quite the party scene we'd left behind, there was still a lot of partying going on downstairs.

One evening, while we were hanging out, one of Paul's friends came by. I couldn't see him clearly at first and just noticed a chubby guy in the doorway. But the moment he stepped into the living room, my jaw dropped. It was my old friend Kenny.

I'd had no idea what had happened to Kenny. When I got out of prison, he was long gone. I heard he'd overdosed and had a stroke, then left Toronto, but I sure didn't know he'd moved to Calgary, much less that he was still hanging out with Paul. But there he was, standing in the living room with a six-pack in his hand, just like all those years before.

Kenny was as shocked as I was when he saw me sitting there. He did a quick double-take and then just said, "Hey, Claire," and nodded, as if we'd just seen each other the day before—not years and a prison stint before.

Kenny had changed profoundly. He'd been in great shape when I knew him, very muscular. But now he was balding and chunky and his face had become rounder, which made it hard to recognize him at all. But the same twinkly blue eyes and lopsided grin broke through his new face, and the biker in him was still there in the way he held himself and talked. He was the same Kenny, I could tell, but older and more damaged.

Kenny stayed for a beer and chatted, but he didn't show much interest in why I was there or what I'd been up to, so I played along and just acted like it was perfectly normal to see him again. I wondered if maybe his memory had been damaged by the overdose and stroke, or maybe the memories were just too hard. Or maybe he just didn't care. Whatever it was, it was a strange and uncomfortable visit, but he didn't stay long. After he finished his beer, he got up and left, as if a whisper from my past had blown through with the wind and then was gone. When the door closed behind him, it was as if a door had closed on my past, and I knew I was moving forward, not lingering in the good ol' party days that may have kept us entertained but did so much damage to our lives.

The summer went by quickly, but the days and nights were endless. Although it was summertime and the best possible time to visit Calgary—since in winter, it could be bone-chilling cold—the sun was incredibly hot. The house was so cramped and messy and chaotic that everyone seemed to be constantly on edge. Everyone but the kids, that is. My daughter was having the time of her life, playing with all the big girls who doted on her, as well as with one of the little boys Joyce watched who was about her age. Those two giggled and played like brother and sister in the little wading pool in the backyard all day long. But all the noise and chaos was driving me mad. It was a relief to leave for work each morning, but coming home at the end of the day was like stepping into a madhouse—hardly the idyllic retreat I'd envisioned when I contemplated returning to the mountains.

Finally, though, we packed the kids in the car, stocked up the ice chest with some food and beer, and hit the road for a day trip to the Rockies. As we drove into the mountains and the air began to cool, I felt my energy returning, fed by the mountain air and the beauty of the mountain peaks topped by dollops of whipped-cream snow.

"Stop!" I suddenly screamed. "Here, right here! Stop the car! This is it!" I didn't mean to scream so loud; it just came out of me, and I startled everyone in the car. Paul swerved onto the skinny shoulder, throwing us all forward in our seats.

"This is where I saw the wild horses!" I shouted, as excited as my daughter had been to see the circus ponies.

"Holy shit, Claire!" Paul yelled at me. "You coulda got us all killed! I thought it was some sort of emergency."

Joyce started cleaning up one of the kids who'd spilled her juice, and another kid started to whine. Everyone in the car seemed upset with me.

"Sorry," I said. "I have to … I have to get out." I looked around to see puzzled, unhappy faces, and I just had to step out of the car. "Let me out. I have to go back there. I have to see if they're still there."

"Claire, that was years ago. Those horses you saw are long gone," Paul said as he started to turn back onto the road.

"No!" I shouted. "Don't leave! They could still be here. I know it; I just know it! Just let us out, and we will go look. You can pick us up on the way back."

"That's crazy," Joyce said. "You can't walk for hours in the wilderness with a two-year-old. You're going to have to do it some other time. That's all there is to it." Her eyes were like steel as they focused on mine, and I knew she was angry. I tried to look away, but I knew she was right, and my eyes filled with tears.

Paul pulled back onto the highway and we drove on, as I stared beyond the rolling hills leading to the mountains, the memories overwhelming me with a sense of something I'd lost before I'd even had it. I pulled my little girl close to me and whispered, "Someday, we'll come back. Someday, we'll find the horses again. Just not today."

After we got back to Calgary, things remained tense, and I knew it was time to go home. Joyce was resentful of the time I was spending with Paul, and one night, she accused me of monopolizing him, which led to a huge fight between us. That was the last straw, I figured, considering I was putting the groceries on her table. So I called into work and left a message saying I wouldn't be back, and I asked Paul to drive us to the airport for a red-eye flight back to Toronto.

After we landed, we grabbed a bright-yellow cab and drove back to our apartment. *This is our world*, I thought as we passed the drab but familiar buildings of the city I'd lived in for years. The energy I had felt in the mountains drained with each block we passed, and by the time we arrived home, I was exhausted. I hadn't really wanted to return to this city, I realized, but I didn't know what else to do. I was tied down and wrapped tightly in the bindings of my past and couldn't quite escape them. Calgary, the mountains, Toronto—all brought back memories that battered me black and blue.

I paid the cabdriver and juggled a two-year-old and all our bags as we walked up the steps to our giant concrete structure of a home. *This is no place to come back to*, I thought. *This is just an empty box we live in. I want to give my little girl something more; I want to see her laughing in the wading pool with other little kids, just like she did in Calgary.* As I put the key into the lock and opened our door, I made up my mind. We'd move in with Shelly and her girls and give it a shot. Maybe together, we'd be able to do more than we could on our own. Maybe we could make a real home for our girls, something neither of us had for ourselves. Maybe together, we could give our girls a family.

Shelly was thrilled with the idea of us moving in. She'd just rented a house in Little Italy, a safe neighborhood in the west end of Toronto, and there was even an extra room. It was the complete opposite of the downtown scene Shelly and I had known so well. The neighborhood was quiet, with many families and parks and playgrounds, and the change in scenery was exciting.

It took about a month to organize the move, and then in a single day, we found ourselves living in our new home, surrounded by boxes waiting to be unpacked. We wandered around the streets of Little Italy, taking in the new neighborhood with the unusual meats hanging in shopkeeper's windows and the smell of fresh pizza permeating the air. It was all so new and exciting, but what I most loved was all the chatter and friendly waves from porches as we passed by. It was a city within a city; only this one was filled with cheerful energy. I was thrilled we'd made the move.

At first, I worried that Shelly might not be accepting of my newfound need to practice a spiritual life. I had to meditate, go to temple, and contemplate in silence. Would that drive her away? I hoped not, because I could not give up this new part of my life, but as time went on, I realized I'd underestimated her, and she really didn't care one way or the other what I believed; she just cared about me. It was a real hard thing to accept at first, that I was worthy of her love and care, but with each day, I learned to open up my heart and trust in my own value.

We slowly established our routines, and as we did, the house became a home. Late at night, after the girls were tucked into their princess beds, Shelly and I would smile together in recognition of what we'd accomplished. We'd done together what no one had ever expected either of us could do. We'd escaped our pasts and started new lives. For ten years, we had lived together in the streets, fighting for survival. Those years may have scarred us both, but they provided a deep sense of understanding between us since we had both suffered so much together. But in our new Little Italy home, we began to create the life we both wanted our girls to have. We took trips to the zoo, threw barbeques in the backyard, and had big sit-down Sunday dinners together.

I moved my piano into the living room and soon spent my evenings playing music by candlelight, a soothing comfort I'd all but given up after Daryl had died. Moving in with Shelly seemed to bring music back into my life, and with it, memories of my loving friend who had died all too soon. Often, in between notes, I would find tears trickling down my face, each drop a tender remembrance of the music we shared together. I even found a stack of music that I'd thought was lost—songs Daryl and I had written at our farm in Northern Ontario. The melodies were even more hauntingly beautiful than when we played them together, and each key I struck opened a tiny crack in my heart. I made a drawer in my Wall just for Daryl, a love gone terribly wrong, and a love that killed two spirits. She had been my mentor and showed me that a life was possible—a real life, a life filled with emotion and music and love. But back then, I wasn't able to understand the duality of life. I didn't understand that without pain, there is no joy. Daryl gave me that one final lesson in her dying; her death brought me incomprehensible pain, a pain that over time helped me to know and feel incomprehensible joy. Playing our haunting songs brought that joy back to me, like a fragrance lingering in the night air, reminding me that even in darkness, there is beauty.

Watching my fingers dance over the keys again also reminded me that I had once been told I'd never play again, after I had sliced open my wrists to ease the pain of living and of watching Daryl dying. But when the doctors told me I'd never play again, I knew I had to prove them wrong. I had to prove to them that I could do and be anything, that my existence mattered. Funny how playing the piano—something I hadn't done in ages until I moved back in with Shelly—had come to symbolize my existence. If I could play, strike the right notes, at just the right time and in just the right combination, I was alive, I mattered. For so long, I had fought the sense that I was disappearing into the world, that I didn't matter. And if I didn't matter, I didn't exist. Isn't that what my birth mother had wished when she gave me away? Or was it what my adopted mother had wished, when she wished me dead?

I had no idea. I only knew that the music that came out of me meant I mattered.

Everything was falling into place, and my life was looking perfect. But on the inside, I didn't feel perfect at all. I was still searching for something, something elusive that seemed to be gnawing at me. On hot, steamy mornings, I would sit on the back step with my coffee and think about the mountains and the wild horses I once knew. It annoyed me that I would continue to obsess about those horses—more specifically, the matriarch, Dali—but after my trip to Calgary, the memory of my morning with the wild horses so many years before had come back to haunt me. Something inside me was missing, something I'd left behind in those mountains: a sense of belonging. No matter how good my life was getting, I felt as if I didn't belong. And Shelly sensed it, too.

The boundaries between life and death are at best shadowy and vague.
Who shall say where one ends and where the other begins?
—Edgar Allen Poe

Chapter 7

Life is a Great Sunrise

There were only a few days until Christmas and presents were piled under the tree, with others hidden away, awaiting Santa's arrival. I was sitting in the admissions office of St. Augustine's Hospital. I was waiting for a little plastic bracelet to identify me by my allergies and room number. Surgery does not accommodate itself to the patient's schedule, as I well knew. My doctor wanted to spend Christmas with his family, so he had planned my hysterectomy right before the holiday so that he would be free to celebrate while I recovered in a hospital bed. It was far from ideal, but I'd been a nurse long enough to know that healthcare has its own timetable and it's best to just accept it. It had taken years of pain and tests to finally accept that I had endometriosis and fibroid tumors. The hidden menaces growing in my uterus had to come out, I knew. I just wanted the pain to be over.

"Don't worry about anything," Shelly told me. "I'll be sure our girls have a great Christmas, and I'll bring her by every day. You just take care of yourself."

I knew the excitement of Santa coming would surpass any worry about my absence. I'd been working in hospitals for a few years by this time and was familiar with the surroundings and procedures, so I wasn't at all nervous. If anything, I was too comfortable, too confident to worry.

The surgery went smoothly and my internal enemies were removed. I celebrated Christmas in my hospital bed surrounded by gifts and laughter. But while I was laughing on the outside, I was silently screaming in agony on the inside. The pain intensified with every breath, until by the time all the guests had left, I knew something just wasn't right and rang for the nurses.

"Oh, that's perfectly normal," a nurse assured me as she busied about my bed, checking my blood pressure and pulse. "It's just gas. It'll clear up."

"No, it's not gas," I told her. "Something's wrong. I know my body, and I'm also a nurse. I'm hurting more than I should be."

She stared at me; her eyes narrowed into small slits of blue, filled with annoyance.

"Don't worry, dear," she said as she pulled the nubby, white bedspread up to my neck as if she'd just as soon strangle me with it. "Remember, you're the patient now. It'll be just fine."

I lay back in bed and felt my abdomen pulse in pain, a pain I knew just wasn't right.

"I'll fix you, Mommy," my little girl told me as she tightly clutched her doctor kit in her arms. She climbed onto the bed and emptied her bag of treasures. "I fix, see." She scattered her instruments across the bedspread: a plastic stethoscope, a huge, pretend syringe, and several Band-Aids, along with a large, plastic thermometer. Her sweet care of me was so funny it hurt. The pain was becoming unbearable, and when I laughed, it was the most excruciating of all. I struggled to hide my pain, to not cry out, and instead I kissed her and thanked her for making my hurt go away. I didn't want her to know how much I was hurting.

But I wanted the nurses to know. An army of sweat beads marched down the sides of my face and joined the ring of dampness around my neck, eventually joining forces with the wet patches under my arms. I was drenched in sweat from the pain. I was hardly recovering; I was getting worse by the minute. When a nurse came in and saw me looking like I'd just had a shower, she was alarmed and shoved a thermometer in my mouth. When I saw the shock on her face, I knew my temperature had spiked to a dangerous level. I remember closing my eyes for a moment, and when I opened them, I saw a group of white coats surrounding my bed.

They were poking and prodding me every which way, talking about my body as if it wasn't attached to me, as if I wasn't even there. I wanted to scream but was too weak to do anything but shoot daggers from my eyes. Some equipment was rolled into the room, and intravenous lines were stuck into both my arms and my ankle. I watched as the white coats left the room as quickly as they entered, when one of the white coats stopped abruptly and turned around.

"You'll be going back into surgery in about an hour to drain an abscess," he said and walked out.

That meant the wound hadn't healed and had instead become infected.

I asked the nurse to bring me the phone, and I called Shelly to tell her what was going on. She put my daughter on the phone and I told her that I loved her, then hung up and dropped the phone beside me and closed my eyes. I wanted to cry, but no tears fell, and I thought that was strange. *Shouldn't I cry?*

I don't really remember being taken to surgery; I was barely aware of what was going on. The next few weeks passed in a blur, and while the world was celebrating the arrival of the New Year, I was having tubes shoved down my nose. I was hooked up to machines that were chirping away, with the bottles filling and emptying with gurgles that sounded to me like death rattles. A doctor told me I had peritonitis and a bowel obstruction. That meant the lining to my abdominal walls had become infected.

I wasn't fine.

The bedside noises assured me I was alive, but I didn't feel very much alive.

I drifted in and out of consciousness; I finally struggled to keep my eyes open long enough to hear what the white coats were saying. They had surrounded my bed and were staring. I wondered what was so interesting. The biggest one, a doctor with a big beard, leaned over so close I could smell his breath. He wasn't doing anything, just staring. My stomach gurgled some more, and the machine chugged up some nasty, brown fecal matter.

The big, bearded doctor rose and took a few steps back, then said, "Listen. Listen carefully. You need to make this decision now." He leaned closer again until his nose was almost touching my own. I wanted to run, to push him off of me and run out the door, away, far away from this place and these white coats and machines. But I couldn't go anywhere. I couldn't even move.

"None of the antibiotics are working," he said. "We've almost run out of options. But we can try a combination of drugs that just might work. It's experimental; we haven't used these drugs in this combination before, but it's our only hope. If we don't try it, you will die. Of course, it's your decision."

"We'll be back in fifteen minutes with some papers for you to sign, and then we'll begin. If that's what you want." Then, as if on

cue, they all turned in a blur of white and left the room. I lay there
alone and wondered if any of it had actually happened or if I was
imagining the whole scene.

"Here. Here, sign here." The charge nurse left a piece of paper
on my chest. I hesitated; I wished there was someone with me who
knew what to do.

"Come on, sign," she ordered as she placed a pen between my
fingers. In the background, I could still hear the doctor's voice, as
if in a whisper: "*You will die. You will die. You will die.*" The nurse
held my hand with the pen inside it and I sloppily signed my name.

"Okay, then, let's get started," she said and turned, the paper
with my signature clutched in her hand. "I'll be right back. Don't
you worry."

How wry.

I lost all sense of time. I was laced up with more tubing, attached
to more machines. I could hear them gurgling and whooshing beside
me. People came and went. I could see their shadows, but I didn't
know who they were. I could hear words, but I didn't know what
they were saying. I felt them touching, prodding me and my belly,
and I wanted to push their hands away, but my arms wouldn't move.
I screamed as loud as I could, over and over, but nobody heard
me. "Leave me alone. Go away. Leave me alone!" I screamed. Why
wouldn't they listen? I couldn't move my lips, but I could hear myself
scream. Surely they heard it, too.

Out of the corner of my eye, I could see the tiny television
hanging from its long arm, as if in midair, suspended over the
gurgling bottles. I looked into the television and could see a picture
of the ocean. I love the ocean. *Listen. Listen to the waves crashing
on the shore, in and out, in and out.* I listened. My energy began to
return. The waves washed away the poisons in my body. *In and out.*

In and out. I wanted to be there, in the ocean, to let the waves carry me out. I wanted the waves to take me to a place of peace.

In and out. In and out. In and out.

Inside my head, I heard the crashing waves and the long whoosh as the ocean pulled them back.

I let myself be pulled into a foamy white wave. It wrapped itself around me and gently pulled me into the depths of the sea. I felt myself rocked in the arms of the ocean. Peace and warmth filled my body, where the icy medicines battled with the pockets of poison in my blood. With each pull further into the dark depth, my pain eased. I was free.

I found myself miles away, yet I could still see the shoreline. The ocean's arms gently rocked me back and forth as I tried to make out what was happening on the shore. A sense of calm filled me with each gentle rocking movement, as the shoreline slowly came into view. It was *me*. It was *me* on the shore. Only it was not *me*, and it was not the shore. It was a shell of me in a bed. My empty shell of an emaciated body lying still on the bed.

The room was silent except for the sounds of the waves as they rolled into the shore. How could that be me? How could I be on the shore and in the bed at the same time? The thought struck me as curious, but nothing more. An overwhelming sense of peace and love swept through me, and I felt an inexplicable sense of oneness with everything. I couldn't stop staring at the shell of myself lying still on the bed. Was I dead?

For the first time ever, I felt safe, warm, and free; I was without physical or emotional pain. When I looked down at the shell, I remembered how cold I was and how much pain I was suffering. The sunken eyes of the shell couldn't possibly be mine.

To the side of the nightstand, I saw a picture, crowded among bottles and jars and Kleenex. A perfect little angel smiled back at me, as if she was waiting for me. She was just smiling and watching, sitting patiently, as if waiting for someone. Her hazel eyes focused on mine, and I knew that she was waiting for me.

I can't leave, I thought. *Not yet. My work isn't finished. There is a purpose in my living.* But I was reluctant to give up the incredible, warm feeling of peace and love. It was what I have always longed for and never found: to be free of pain and to know that I am loved.

I couldn't take my eyes off of the calm little girl on the night table, smiling with her hazel eyes.

I heard myself screaming for help.

Instantly, I was returned to the shell body. My eyes were startled open by alarms screaming into the silent hospital night. In seconds, my room was crowded and everyone was talking at once.

"Get off of me! Get off!" It felt like a thousand horses pounding on my chest with their hooves. I thought I was silently screaming, but that wasn't possible. Tubes running down my throat blocked my mouth. My eyes became wild and frantically moved back and forth in fear. I felt like an animal, trapped and terrified.

"It's okay. You'll be fine. You gave us a scare, but it's all right now," a nurse said as she gently wiped my brow with a warm cloth. "Try to relax. You almost didn't come back to us."

I searched her eyes for answers. *Back from where?* I wondered.

I had no sense of time. I was weak and filled with the poison from all the plastic bags. Each time I let my eyes close, time traveled without me. I was aware of the noises around me. I heard the alarms going off and the soft, pumping breaths coming from the machines, as if they, too, were alive. I could hear the gentle reassurances from the nurses as they washed my face and rolled me over. I felt the white coats stare as they surrounded my bed and discussed my body. Each day, I felt longer surges of awareness and my strength returning. Eventually, I was lucid, and I was moved to the regular floor to begin the process of resurfacing.

No one spoke of what had happened. I was only assured that they thought they'd lost me, but I came back. When I tried to learn more, the subject was changed. The white coats seemed pleased with themselves as they nodded their heads and congratulated each other on their choices of medications. The poisons they chose were eradicating the infections.

The doctors and nurses had saved my life.

I stopped asking questions and was just filled with gratitude for what they had done, and for the chance I'd been given to return to the world. I wanted to give back, to use my second chance at life to help others. I was reborn.

I am alone; I am always alone, no matter what.
—Marilyn Monroe

Chapter 8

Anyone Out There?

The night I came home, Shelly cried. In all the years I'd known her, I'd never seen her cry.

"I was so scared," she said. "I thought you were going to die."

"Yeah, well, a lot of our friends have died," I reminded her. "It wouldn't have been a big deal." Of course, I knew it would have been a huge deal to the kids, but Shelly would have gotten over it in no time, I figured.

"Fuck you," she answered, growing angry. "Do you have *any* idea how much you matter? To the girls, to me, to all of your friends?"

"No," I said honestly. I really didn't understand. What difference would it have made to my friends if I had died? I made no real impact on anyone's life but my daughter's. I knew if I died, my friends' lives would go on and they'd forget about me soon enough.

Somehow, I seemed to have already lost the wisdom I'd gained in the hospital. Back home and returned to my life, I wasted no time in resorting back to the belief that I didn't matter to anyone, ever. I was born to be discarded, passed on to someone else. That was an identity I just couldn't shake, no matter what anyone said otherwise.

I searched Shelly's eyes for understanding, and I saw none. She didn't understand why I didn't understand. And so we lived together, each sequestered in our own worlds, as winter turned into spring, and then into summer. By the fall, we'd grown so estranged that there was no sense in sharing the same house. So one day, without any warning, I packed our things, and with only a few dollars in my pocket, said good-bye to Shelly and the girls, and we moved away.

Just like that. It was fast and furious and everyone was really upset—Shelly with me, the girls with me. But I'd had enough of living there, and I knew it was only a matter of time before Shelly wanted me gone anyway. That may not have been the case, but at the time, I was so convinced she'd eventually want to be rid of me that I was going to beat her to it.

I rented an apartment on Christie Street, not too far away. We hadn't been there long when I heard that a friend of mine, Brian, had saved a boy's life. I knew Brian from the downtowner days; we had lived in the same high-rise that housed people in little boxes. We both chose to pursue our dreams—I went into nursing, and he became an emergency medical technician (EMT) and moved to the Philippines. It was there that he saw a young boy in the ocean being sucked out to sea and he leapt in and saved him.

I was so proud of Brian; he'd had a really rough life, and he really struggled to make something of his life. Learning that he would risk his own life to save someone else's didn't surprise me. That was the kind of man he was, and that was why he was one of my best friends.

Shortly after hearing about his heroics, however, another tragedy showed up on my doorstep like a dead bird. It was Brian's brother, and I was delighted to see him. I invited him inside, and we sat at the kitchen table having coffee and chatting about what we'd been up to since we'd last met.

"Here, I brought you some pictures," he said, spreading out a bunch of glossy color photos on my kitchen table. At first, I just saw some smiling pictures of Brian and was thinking they'd be pictures of him in the Philippines, but then I saw a photo of a coffin and a parade of people holding banners over their heads. And on the banners was written Brian's name, and on top of the coffin was a giant photo of his face.

"What do you think you're doing?" I screamed at his brother. I didn't know what kind of sick joke he was pulling, or why, but I sure didn't like it. "Why are you showing me this? Is this a joke?" Tears were running down my face as I realized it was no joke. Brian was dead.

"I'm sorry," his brother said gruffly, gathering all the photos into a stack, "I thought you knew. Brian died in the Philippines. He killed himself."

In an instant, my body shrank into itself, and a powerful grief swept through me. I couldn't believe it. Brian couldn't be dead. He had just saved a boy's life—why in the world would he have killed himself?

But at the same time, I knew it was true. Brian had a dark side. He spoke to me of suicide often, but once he had found his calling as an EMT, I was certain those feelings had left him.

And the knowledge that they hadn't made me wonder how far away I myself was from all the self-destructive behaviors overtaking me. A familiar deep, animal growl began churning in my throat, trying to escape, wanting its freedom. I wanted to scream, to howl, to roar at the world, but I wouldn't allow myself to do that. Not in front of this man I barely knew.

I took a deep breath and tried to steady myself as his words slowly sunk into my mind and I could hear them.

"I don't know the details, but I'm going tomorrow to find out," he was saying.

"Going where?" I said, shaking myself into the present.

"The Philippines," he said, the note of irritation in his voice suggesting I hadn't been paying attention. "I'm going to find out what happened, why he killed himself. At least, that's what Interpol said."

I couldn't accept it. Maybe Interpol was lying. Maybe someone killed him.

But I knew I'd never find the answer. I knew because I already had the answer. Brian was dead. That was all I needed to know.

I had lost another friend.

And now I was so afraid I might lose myself. If Brian couldn't make it in the real world, could I? Here I was, at the end of another decade of my life, having survived so many losses and wounds, but no matter how far I came, I still felt completely alone in the world, except for my little girl. With Brian gone, and Daryl gone, and so many other friends gone, even Shelly—who had been newly diagnosed with cancer and from whom I was still estranged since I left—I really was alone. Utterly, completely alone, just as I had been the day I was born and unaccepted.

I had to find my acceptance. I had to find out where I came from, before I could ever really know where I was going.

Until then, I quietly tucked Brian into my Wall of Secrets, where our many secrets we had shared would rest in peace.

On my thirtieth birthday, I called Parent Finders. It was an organization that helped connect adoptees with their birth parents.

"And do you have any information about your birth parents?" the woman on the other end of the phone asked me.

"No, I don't know anything," I said, "But I suspect my adoptive mother knows. Whenever I raised the subject, she changed it, but it's pretty clear she knows."

"I'm afraid we can't really help you without more information," the woman told me. "But if you can talk to your mother and get her to share what she knows with you, then call us back and we'll see what we can do."

"I've tried that and she won't tell me."

"Then all I can suggest is get a lawyer."

I had no money for a lawyer. Which meant I had to call my mother.

"I don't know what you're talking about," she said.

"I want to know the name of my birth mother," I said again. This time, she paused, as if to consider it. "It was all so long ago, I don't remember those kinds of details."

That was the closest she'd ever come to admitting I was adopted.

"Those kinds of details? Mom, that's not a little detail. I know you know, and I want you to tell me."

"Why? You don't think she wants to hear from you, do you? She didn't raise you; I did. I don't know why you need to be looking for someone who didn't even want you."

That stung, but I wasn't going to give up, just because she was so good at manipulating people by striking at their soft spots. "If you don't tell me, I'll get a lawyer and I'll take you to court," I said. "And then it will be public record. Everyone in Belleville will know the truth." Even though I couldn't afford a lawyer, I knew if I struck at her soft spot—her reputation—she'd be the one to give up.

"I'm not making any promises," she said, clearly conceding. "I'll think about it; that's all. But if you know what's good for you, you'll give up this ridiculous idea of yours right now and stop trying to find the woman who gave you up. She didn't want you then, so she's sure not going to want you now."

I hung up the phone and cried.

A week later, an envelope arrived. It was from my mother, and for the first time, I was thrilled to hear from her. I ripped the letter opened, and all that was in it was a small scrap of paper, just a little piece that had been ripped from a bigger sheet. And on it was written a single name. A surname. That was all. No note, no explanation, nothing, just a surname. But it was an unusual one, and it was the biggest clue I'd ever had.

I held the little scrap of paper in my hand and stared and stared. It was my first glimpse of who I was, my identity, in a surname.

It felt absolutely amazing.

I walked in circles, around and around the living room, and said the name out loud. Over and over, as if trying on a new coat made of letters, the letters to my name. They didn't fit, but maybe that was because the coat was new; it needed breaking in. I had to wear it.

But maybe the name didn't fit because that wasn't who I was. That family gave me away, after all. I wasn't good enough for them to keep. As the self-defeating thoughts swirled, new emotions emerged—pain, which was of course familiar, but now it was mixed with hope. I opened up a beer and drank it down, and then another and another. By the time I'd gone through enough beers to calm myself, I'd also emboldened myself.

"Only one way to find out why they didn't want me," I declared to my final beer. "Call 'em!"

But how, who? Where to begin? With the operator, of course.

I dialed the operator and explained my situation. The operator was very understanding, and she looked up the name. There were about fifteen of them, scattered across the country.

"Call 'em all!" I declared to one more beer. I decided to start close to home.

"Hello, you don't know me, but—"

But before I could finish, the phone was either hung up or I was told, "We aren't interested."

So I tried another approach.

"Hello, my name is Claire Hitchon, and I am looking for my birth family." It was perhaps a bit too direct for an introduction, but no one hung up when they heard that.

But I found myself tearing up with the first few calls. All I was met with were evasive words coated with a frosting of understanding. Each person I talked to was uncomfortably certain that no one in his or her family had given any babies away.

When I'd gone through all the possibilities that were close to home, I tried the names in more distant places. I called people in every major city heading west across Canada. Finally, my hope dying like the flickering flame of a candle burning out, I tried Vancouver, on the other side of my world. There were a few of my surnames there, and I looked at the numbers, closed my eyes, and let my finger do the walking.

Eenie, meenie, miney, moe. With this last one, I shall go …

I opened my eyes and saw that my finger had landed on a name at the top of the list. I dialed each digit as I listed to the musical sound the dial pad made as it moved back to the top, my heart beating so loudly that it almost drowned out the sounds of the dial. With the receiver squished against my ear, I was lost in the land of eternal ringing, and it took me a few seconds to register that a voice was asking me something. I muttered an apology and began my life story, which had shortened considerably from my first few calls to my fifteenth call.

"You know, that sounds like it could be my aunt," a young woman said. "She lives in Alberta, and she's divorced with three kids. I can't say for sure, but let me talk to my dad about it. Can you call back next week and maybe I'll have something for you?"

I couldn't believe my ears! After all these years of not knowing who I was or where I'd come from, I was finally coming close to finding my birth family!

"Of course. Sure, sure. Whatever you want. I will. I can't wait. I'm so excited. You could be part of my family!" My high-pitched squeal was annoying even to me, but before I could apologize for that, too, the dial tone abruptly silenced me. It was the only conversation I had ever had with someone who could be my family, and it was over, just like that. But I had the number, and I was told to call back in a week, so that was exactly what I'd do. I'd waited this long to know my true family; I could wait another week.

Or so I thought.

It was the longest week of my life. I marked each day off of my calendar, and with each big *X*, my heart became more alive with excitement, and hope began to return to my life.

When seven days had passed, I sat down to the table where the telephone was and arranged it for the call. I cleared off the junk mail, put all my pens and pencils in the little porcelain jar on the desk, got a pad of paper and pen ready in case I needed anything, and poured a glass of water. Then I picked up the phone, eager to dial the numbers that would change my life forever.

I dialed each digit; my fingers anxiously hovered above the rotary dial as I watched each number spin back into its place. Finally, after what seemed an eternity, the numbers were all dialed, and I placed the phone against my ear to await the big news. Was her aunt my birth mother?

"We're sorry, but the number you have reached is not in service," the recorded voice informed me. "Please check the number you have dialed."

I carefully rechecked the number and redialed. Three times. And three more times, I was told that they'd disconnected their telephone.

I felt utterly destroyed.

There is nothing like returning to a place that remains unchanged
To find the ways in which you yourself have altered.
—Nelson Mandela

Chapter 9

Full Circle

For years, she sent the letters. And for years, I'd tear them up. Ever since my mother had declared she'd wished I'd died, the letters would arrive, filled with venomous hate, telling me how I was the spawn of the devil, that I was a sinner like the woman who'd given birth to me and that I would burn in hell. Her words of hate dressed in religious garb just got crazier and crazier as the years went on. Eventually, when they would arrive in their familiar handwriting from that familiar Belleville address from my unhappy past, I would tear them up without even opening them.

But that day, for some inexplicable reason, I didn't tear the letter up. There was something about it that was different. This one was in a smaller envelope, and the handwriting was different in some way. Her usual hate mail was typewritten and filled large envelopes, leaving no space around the paper's edges. This one also wasn't thick like usual. It wasn't a manifesto, but a note. I held it up to the light, and the outline of a tiny piece of paper showed through. The temptation was too great not to tear it open. I got my letter opener and sat down at the table. I didn't want to be standing in case it knocked me down.

The sound of ripping paper sent a shiver through me—opening it meant risking reading something cruel and vicious. But I was just too curious to do otherwise. Within seconds, the tiny piece of paper inside the envelope fluttered out and over the table. My eyes followed it, the way I might follow a feather falling to the ground. *Maybe I won't have to touch it at all* I thought, *if it lands right side up.* Maybe I wouldn't burn my fingers with her hatred if I didn't have to touch it.

The next few minutes seemed to unfold in slow motion as the paper landed facedown on the table. I took the tip of a pen, flipped it over, and leaned closer toward it, so that I could read its single line, written in a shaky hand.

Your father is dying. He has cancer.

Nothing more. I read the words over and over, trying to understand what I was supposed to do. Was I supposed to rush home? Was I supposed to rush to his bedside when the only words at my own bedside were that my mother wished I were dead? How could she expect anything from me after the way she had treated me over the years?

Still, my father was not my mother. He was a gentle spirit with a kind heart, whose only real wrongdoing was to be intimidated by her. He loved children and animals; she had nothing but contempt for them. He had wanted a child; she had not. She should never have been given one.

My father had always wanted a son, however, not a daughter. She, who was unable to bear children, had reluctantly agreed to an adoption, but of a boy, not a girl, whom she would have seen as competition for her husband's attention. A girl might one day grow up to be prettier than she, just when she was growing older; a girl would be more difficult for her to manipulate, given her mastery of men.

But there were no available boys, just me, of the inferior gender. After much persuasion, she agreed to take me in, on sort of a loaner plan. If a boy became available within the first two years of my life, she would not finalize the adoption; she'd exchange me for a boy.

Unfortunately for me, they never brought her a boy.

But my father loved me. He may have preferred a boy, but like so many parents, he loved the child he had, regardless of my genitalia. And he would love to be around my daughter. He had only met his granddaughter in secret, as my mother had told everyone I was dead. Even those meetings were very infrequent. I knew that he would adore her.

But he'd never even know her, unless I brought her to him.

The reality of his dying slowly seeped into my soul. He would be gone; he would never know this sweet little girl, and my sweet little girl would never know him. If only it could be different. If only we could have a normal family, with a grandpa to play with. He could teach her to fish, like he taught me. She could sit in his big leather chair, just like I did. She could play with his whiskers and fall asleep on his lap. He could tell her stories she'd remember the rest of her life. If only she could meet him.

Tears began to fall from my face and onto the slip of paper as I imagined a different life, a life filled with family and love. Could we have it? Was it even possible that she and I and my father might know a few months, maybe even a few years, of precious joy?

The moments of joy I'd had with my father began to return; they were few, and the memories flowed through me like a sweet river of happiness, as the image of my mother disappeared from my view. I wanted to see him. I needed to see him. And he and my little girl deserved a relationship, whether or not my mother and I had a bad one.

What was I thinking? Was I actually imagining returning to Belleville? Not just for a visit, but for whatever time my father had left?

Yes, I was. And as the idea of moving back to the place of secrets sunk in, every ounce of my energy drained from me. My heart was heavy with pain as moment by moment, the memories of my childhood that I'd locked away in the Wall of Secrets flickered into my conscious mind. The beatings that had been silent for so long began to awaken. The hateful words of my mother screamed in my ears. And the rapes that I suffered when I fled from her home came back like a bullwhip, whipping me into submission.

I breathed in, and my nostrils burned with the smell of cancer as it had eaten away at the flesh of my friend Daryl. The same smell would surround my father. My mother's words of hate forced themselves into my thoughts; they fought for acknowledgment as I tried to focus on my dad. My worlds were battling for victory— victory over my mother by never returning, and victory over my mother by returning—to not let her win and keep my daughter and me from my dad. My body swayed as it was pulled in both directions, and the screams inside my head sent shivers up my spine. The battle was mine alone to conquer.

The reality was that my daughter would benefit from getting out of the city. I had always wanted to raise her in a smaller community, and Belleville was just the right size and surrounded by nature. And the reality was that she would benefit from knowing her grandpa.

As the battle waged inside my head, I shoved my fears back into a drawer in the Wall of Secrets. I couldn't focus on myself any longer;

I had to focus on my daughter and my dying father. The circle of my life had returned to where the journey began.

I'd made my decision. We would move to Belleville.

When I called my mother, I expected her to slam the phone down, but this time, she didn't. After a few of her perfunctory insults, I took control of the conversation.

"What kind of cancer does he have? How far advanced is it? Is he under treatment?"

"Your father has bladder cancer," she said, "and yes, it's advanced. They aren't sure how much longer he has."

"Yes, but what stage is it at? What kind of treatment is he getting?"

"He's getting perfectly fine treatment. I don't know why you would ask that kind of a question, unless you think I would prevent him from getting treatment," she responded, trying to turn a reasonable question into an argument. But I wasn't biting. I realized the only way I'd know for sure how my father was doing would be to go down there myself and find out.

"Mom, we are moving back to Belleville to take care of him."

"What? You are doing no such thing. I am perfectly capable of taking care of him myself."

"I know you are, but I want to see my father, and I want my daughter and Dad to get to know each other before he dies. I'm not asking your permission, Mother; I'm telling you that this is what I've decided. We'll get an apartment, but I would appreciate if we could stay with you for a week or two while I look for something."

I heard her breathing loudly, contemplating what to say. Finally, she let out a deep breath, as if in resignation, and said, "Well, I suppose you can stay in the upstairs apartment. We converted the upstairs to rentals a few years ago, and there's an empty one you can rent."

"That sounds great," I said as I wondered if it was really a great idea to live so close. But I was so overwhelmed with the move that the idea of having a place ready to rent, and near my dad, sounded perfect.

"But you aren't staying for free," she said. "I expect you to pay rent."

"That's fine," I said.

"And help out around the house. I'm not putting up with any freeloading. I expect you to carry your weight around here."

"I will," I said, exhaling in exasperation myself at her negativity.

"And that child of yours had better behave," she added.

"She's a sweet girl, and Dad is going to love getting to know her," I said as I wrapped up the conversation. What in the world was I getting myself into?

As I boxed up our lives, I stacked them neatly around our apartment and watched them grow higher and higher. Somewhere, as I hid behind that fortress of a boxed-up life, I hid my reluctance. Each box became a barrier to my pain as I placed it on the stack, as if the higher I piled them, the harder it would be for that pain to reach me. But some days, each piece of tape I put on a box felt like the nails to my coffin.

When the school year ended, just after my daughters seventh birthday, we said good-bye to Little Italy and hello to the little city on the lake where I'd grown up and now, for a while at least, so would she. My nerves were strung so tightly that if I was a guitar string, I'd have snapped before a single note had played. I was entering the vortex of my past and the swiftly moving current of my future. And it scared the shit out of me.

When we reached Belleville, I was startled by how much the house had changed. Just as my mother had said, the upstairs had been converted into two apartments. To replace the loss of bedrooms, however, they had converted my beloved library into a master bedroom. I was devastated to realize I would never again sit in the library where my Wall of Secrets had been. For that matter, I would never again see my Wall of Secrets. She'd sold it.

Even though I was back in my childhood home, I no longer had my sacred space, or my secret space. I would have to retain my Wall of Secrets in my own imagination, where I knew they would be safe from her prying eyes.

As for the kitchen, it had been expanded and updated to my mother's specifications, with a huge picture window where she could sit in her rocking chair and admire the gardens and lilacs she so carefully looked after. I hadn't been there a day before it was apparent that the spot had become her post. She could watch the neighbors and note when they left and what or whom they brought home. If someone had a new car or a new hat or a curious friend, she knew about it first. And if someone came to visit her, she was able to see who came down the long driveway before they even noticed her sitting there. Sitting in her rocking chair, she could guard her treasures and keep her world safe from the privacy of her own kitchen.

"You're going to have to take all those boxes upstairs yourself," she said and then added, "and when you're done, we can go over the rules. You do know about rules, don't you, both of you?" she asked, hoping no doubt that my daughter wouldn't know what a rule was. My mother was so certain my little girl would be an out-of-control child that it almost seemed to fluster her when she found herself looking at an adorable, well-behaved little girl.

"Yes," She answered softly, cautious to not upset this strange lady that was her grandma.

"Very good. Well, you help your mother take her things upstairs, and when you're done, I'll fix you a sandwich. And then we can go over the house rules. Rules are very important, and in this house, if you don't follow them, you will not be able to stay here. Do you understand?"

"Yes, I understand."

"All right then, run along." She forced her mouth into a tight smile, which came across more like a grimace of pain. *It probably does hurt her to smile*, I thought as I took my daughter by the hand.

"Come on, honey, let's get these things into our new apartment!" I did my best to be light and happy so that she wouldn't be too scared, but she sensed my own fears and no doubt had some of her own right off the bat since she had met my mom.

"Your father is taking a nap, so don't make any noise," she screeched as we went outside to the moving truck and started to unload our old life and move it into our new life.

My father never said much. She was the one who did all the talking, and he just followed along. He was happy to see me and pleased he'd be able to spend time with his granddaughter, but we weren't there long before she dominated our daily lives. While I took my father to his doctor appointments, accompanied him to chemotherapy and his surgeries, treated his surgical wounds and dispensed his medication, she made sure none of her rules were violated. My little girl learned quickly not to touch Grandma's things, not to get her fingerprints on anything, not to track mud into the house. She learned how to set the table precisely, how to address Grandma, and how to polish the silver. I learned how to control my temper.

Most of the time.

But sometimes, I couldn't take it. She was watching us constantly, shushing and cautioning and criticizing every time she opened her mouth. My parenting, my choices, even my growing desire to go back to school and get my RN degree, all became opportunities to find fault. Nothing had changed since I'd left fifteen years before. Not even the summer cottage.

My parents had several cottages at Oak Lake, and every summer, we would go there for a "vacation." It wasn't a place for fun; it was a place for work. From the minute we got there to the minute we left, I worked. Each cottage needed to be scraped and painted on rotation. That meant every summer, there was a cottage that had to be painted. And they all had to have the windows washed and pine needles that had fallen from the trees outside raked into neat piles—her way, of course, always her way.

She began as soon as we got there. "You can do the raking while your mother scrapes the paint. I'll keep an eye on Grandpa."

"Okay, Grandma," My daughter obediently said, clearly unhappy.

"She can help with the raking, but I'd like her to spend some time playing first," I said. I had no intention of turning the summer trip to the lake into an ordeal of hard labor for my daughter. I wasn't going to let her live the life I'd lived.

"She's old enough to pitch in like everybody else," my mother declared.

"She can pitch in, but she's a child, and children need to play," I countered.

"I'm not having any kids run wild up here. We have tenants who come here to relax." Her voice began its high-pitched squeal that sounded to me like nails on a chalkboard.

"No, Mother!" I shouted. My head was boiling, I was so angry. "She is not going to be your servant!"

My sweet girl started to tear up, and I knew it was already out of my hands. I was furious, and I wanted to let my mother have it.

"I will not have you talk to me that way," my mother ordered; she feared she was losing control of the argument, while I was afraid I was losing control of my temper.

"You two, knock it off," my dad said, startling us both. "My granddaughter and I are going to go down to the lake and catch some fish, aren't we?" His smile turned her tears into a big grin.

"Yeah, Poppa!" she said. "Let's catch some fish for supper!"

The two of them headed to the lake to go fishing, and I knew that whatever the arguments between me and my mother, it was worth it just to see her have some adventures with her Poppa.

After they left, my mother and I went back to screaming and slamming doors, and I got ready to scrape the goddamned paint.

The next day, I made some phone calls and requested the application materials to go back to school and get my nursing degree. If we were ever going to get out from under my mother's watch, I would have to be able to earn a decent living. I was determined to get my degree and make a better home for my daughter than my mother had ever made for me.

We stayed in the "upper cottage" and my parents in the larger "lower" one. We spent our days trying to accommodate her list of things to be done, while my father just got sicker. His once-large frame was shrinking more and more each day, and his eyes had become dull and sunk into a pale, worn face. But on good days, he made sure to enjoy every last bit of time he had left, and that was mostly with his fishing buddy.

They spent their time at the water's edge, she floating around in an old inner tube, talking a mile a minute, him smoking his cigarettes, carefully blowing the smoke out of the right side of his mouth so that my mom couldn't see it from the front windows. We all knew she kept an eagle eye on him—to be sure he didn't violate any of the laws she'd set down for him decades before, laws that defined how their lives would be lived.

I'd wander down to check on them whenever I could, walking down the path to the water where, from the distance, I could see his once-white hair shimmering with a yellowish tinge, his shoulders hunched over as he sat on the old leather bench he'd made from the backseat of an old Volkswagen. They would usually be deep in conversation about such things as the sunfish and their houses or the weeds and how they grew only in certain places. The fish nests intrigued her and she would put her face into the water and blow bubbles so she could look at them closer through the round swirls of sand created by mother fishes to protect their spawn.

"Look, Poppa!" she would call to him, "Watch me! I can dive! See? Poppa, are you watching?"

"I am; I am." His reply would be weak and wheezy, and my heart ached to see him struggle through his pain to play with his little granddaughter.

But back at the cottages, where my mother orchestrated the chores, another scene was playing out.

As she instructed me about what needed to be done and how to do it, my rage would build, and eventually, it would always erupt. I couldn't control my anger around her no matter how hard I tried— and to tell the truth, I didn't try too hard around her. I was filled with resentment at her flagrant hostility and determination to quash the joy out of everyone around her. Before long, we would both be screaming at each other through the silence of the pines. It got to the point where even I was worried about what the neighbors would think; we were so filled with mutual rage. It was as if time had gone backward and I was once again the age my daughter was now.

I was grown now, and my mother was creeping into old age as my father slowly died. Yet still, we were screaming the same words, the same hatred. The only difference was that now I was fighting back, which just amplified the hatred. Years of our frustrations and anger spewed from us until we were both reduced to our wounds and our rage.

"You never could do anything right!" she screamed again and again as she stood there in her apron, her hands on her hips in the exact same posture she'd struck years before, screaming the exact same words. Only now, her hair was white, her balance unsteady. "I don't know why you had to come back here. I told you the rules, and yet you still insist on doing everything you can to upset your father and me. Just do what I ask, with no questions—and do it right!"

Her eyes would bulge out from the fish-eye lenses of her glasses, and I swear, I could feel the negative energy radiating from her skin. Every day passed like that, every day with a screaming argument that ended up with her crying and screaming as I held my ground and fought back. I would not give in to her demands just because she made them. I was going to let her know that I was the one who was strong now. I was the one raising a daughter, and I was the one taking care of my dad.

She was the one who wished me dead.

It had been a really bad day. Another scream fest between me and my mom, and neither of us would give in. All I could think about was packing our bags and getting out of there, but I had no idea where we'd go. And I couldn't leave my dad, especially if it meant leaving him alone with her. At least his granddaughter gave him a diversion from his illness, and I was able to be sure he was comfortable and getting proper treatment. Left alone with her, there was no telling what he'd endure.

I was sitting at the antique table in my "upper cottage," tracing the flowers on the old, white plastic tablecloth, wondering what I should do, as the tears fell from my face like rain.

My little sweetheart was making mud pies in her restaurant down by the lake, singing away as if she didn't have a care in the world except how her pies would turn out and whether we would come and sample them.

The screen door squeaked as it opened, announcing a visitor. As I turned my head and wiped my eyes with a napkin, I prayed it wasn't my mother.

It was my father.

When I turned and saw him standing there in the sunlight, just as I'd seen him stand so many times when I was a little girl, looking up to him in the cottage after a long day of cleaning, scraping, and painting, I was struck by how old and sick he had become. I knew he'd had blood in his urine for some time now, which wasn't a good sign at all. It meant the tumors were growing. Soon, they would fill his whole bladder, and it would have to be removed. Then he'd need someone to help clean the stoma, change the bags—tasks I knew would be beneath the dignity of my mother.

As he stood there, a sense of shame came over me as I realized I had just been contemplating leaving him with her.

Without saying a word, he pulled out a chair and sat down with a painful grunt.

His hand reached into his tattered shirt pocket and he pulled out his package of tobacco and rolling papers, and with shaky hands, he placed them on the table. His skin had become so loose and wrinkled, and a stroke he'd had before I got there had left one of his arms nearly immobile. He held it to his side almost as if it were in an invisible sling. He laid the arm on the table, where it lay limp, like it belonged to someone else.

I looked into my father's watery blue eyes as if seeing them for the first, and perhaps last, time. They were a paler blue than I remembered, and I wondered if I'd just remembered them wrong, or if their color was fading along with his spirit. Loose bags of skin hung under them, empty of the flesh they once held. His yellowing white hair hung in strings around his face, a face that had become covered in large sunspots and scars from where melanomas had been removed over the years.

Weathered was the word that came to mind. My father's face was weathered, but behind those watery eyes, I saw fear and pain. He was dying, and he was hurting, and he was in pain.

"Your mother's upset," he said as he rolled a cigarette with his shaking hands. "Again."

"Here, let me roll some," I said, taking the pouch of tobacco and the papers and filling them expertly, having watched him roll them for years and honing my skills in prison. Neither of us wanted to look at the other, so both of us rolled and smoked in silence. It had become our common bond since I'd returned, the thread that tied our conversations together when words became obstacles for us to stumble upon.

My father was a man of few words, so I knew that however silent he might be, by coming in and sitting down, he was communicating something important.

"I can't take it anymore, Claire. The yelling. Her crying. No more." His words were uttered without emotion, and his face was turned away as he smoked his cigarette. "Please, for me. Stop fighting with her. I just can't take anymore."

His words struck my heart. I knew how much it took for him to say something. He had always fallen silent in the face of our battles, not from accepting her side, but from not wanting to enflame the fire any further. To ask me to stop was to put the burden on me to be the peacemaker, even if he knew it wasn't me who had waged war all these years.

Our eyes connected briefly. "Okay," I said. "For you, I'll try. But you know how she is. She's so hurtful. It's hard to ignore it."

"I know. But do it for me. Please." He pushed himself up with his one good arm, turned, and walked out, letting the screen door slam shut behind him.

I was losing my father. The one ally I had in the Hitchon world, and I was losing him to cancer, maybe even losing him to the war of words between my mom and me. My greatest fear was coming true.

He was leaving me. I had always prayed that my mother would go first, but I knew that wouldn't happen. I was going to have to live in my worst nightmare: my mother and I, alone.

There are as many pillows of illusion as flakes in a snowstorm.
We wake from one dream into another dream.
—Ralph Waldo Emerson

Chapter 10

It's a Fine Line

It was early March when the letter arrived. It was from the nursing school, and I prepared myself for rejection. Although in my former program, my grades had been good and my test scores high, I had a terrible fear that this school would have discovered my past, known about the jail sentence, and refused to even consider me. It was as if I were living a dual life and they'd somehow know who I "really" was—the damaged Claire, the junkie Claire, the Claire I'd put away into my drawer of secrets. My entire past, from the time of my conception, had somehow shadowed my life and blanketed the goodness, the achievements, and my determination to succeed in a caul of darkness. Anything positive about my life was clouded by the sense that I was worthless. And I just knew that letter I held in my hand would be one more blow.

But I was wrong. I'd been accepted.

I was thrilled when in the fall, my daughter and I both started school. She was entering the third grade, and at long last, I was entering the RN program to become a registered nurse.

When she got home from school, my mother would be there to put her to work and, hopefully, make her a snack. If I had to study late, she would fix dinner for her and my father, but most of the time, I fixed it when I got home.

I rarely ate with my parents. I just couldn't afford the stress of being around my mother. Just coexisting in the same house was a challenge, and I noticed that I was becoming weaker and sicker myself, the more time I spent around her. It was as if my body was absorbing her bitterness, dissolving from the acids of her heart. I had to stay away to survive.

I studied and worked for hours into the night, stopping only long enough to tuck my daughter in to bed and read her a bedtime story. I wanted to spend more time with my little girl, but I knew that if I was going to be able to give her a better life, I had to get my nursing degree. And so studying became a desperate passion, as I grew more and more determined to give her all that I didn't have.

I wanted her to have a place to call home where should could have her friends over to play—rather than a monument to social status, where children weren't allowed.

I wanted her to have a bedroom she could call her own, where she could fall asleep feeling safe and protected from harm—a room where she could put her posters of rock stars and artwork on the walls, a place of peace that was all hers.

And I wanted her to have music lessons and to be involved in Brownies and Girl Guides and swimming and camp—all things I could not afford as a nursing assistant.

But it all came at a price, a price I could never get back. My time. I had to devote almost all my time to studying and going to school.

On the rare occasions when we would all have dinner together, my father sitting in his usual place in front of the bookcases in his old, worn captain's chair, I would look around the table and wonder how it came to be that I was sitting at the very same table, in the very same place, eating off of the very same dishes as I had when I was my daughter's age. How was it possible that I had come full circle, only to begin again in the very same place I'd started?

It wasn't long before I'd started school that my father had been diagnosed with Parkinson's disease, and his trembling hands soon turned to trembling and twitching limbs that he so desperately wished he could control. The once-distinguished air force officer now struggled to feed himself as he tried to get a shaking fork into his mouth without the food falling onto his lap. His personality began changing as well. His temper became shorter, and for the first time, he began snapping at my mother or me. He spent his days resting, watching television, or wandering around the back garden, rolling his cigarettes.

After dinner each night, he would make his way outside for an after-dinner smoke, hiding behind the bushes so she wouldn't see him and start nagging.

"Frank," she'd say, pinching her lips together. "You know that's what caused your cancer, don't you?"

"Oh, for Pete's sake," he'd say, "leave me alone!" And off he'd go to smoke his cigarette in peace.

I hated watching him put up with that at the end of his life. If he couldn't enjoy a cigarette in his own backyard in peace, what dignity did he have in his own home? Then one day, right before Christmas, I finally snapped. She had just shrieked her favorite line about how his smoking was the cause of his bladder cancer and he ignored her and put on his heavy jacket to go outside and have a smoke.

The jacket must have weighed more than he did by that point, and watching him head out into the snow to smoke in peace and quiet, weighed down by that coat and her anger, was just too much for me.

"Jesus Christ," I said. "Can't you just let the man smoke in the house in peace, where he's warm and safe? He's dying, and you're still nagging him to quit. I can't believe you have no compassion at all. You're so worried about the smell instead of him. I'm fucking done with it all!"

As I rose to leave, she responded with, "Do the dishes before you storm out of here. And you"—turning to my daughter—"go practice your piano."

The sound of the smacking pointer that I remembered from my childhood came back into my mind the moment she said that. My mother had been teaching her the basics, just as she had taught so many students in years past, but fortunately, she no longer had the pointer to smack her with.

And so she smacked her with words—words meant for me, not for my little girl.

"Do your own damned dishes," I said and then looked at my daughter. "Come on, let's go make a snowman."

We left her sitting in her rocking chair, glaring at the world she could not longer control.

When Christmas came, the tension mounted. Every Christmas with my mother had always been a monumental test of endurance. Her obsession with rules turned into an obsession with blame for anyone violating any rule. All the rules she'd ever had were magnified a thousand times, and the slightest hint that someone might deviate from her strict and endless litany of prohibitions and demands was cause for catastrophe. And this Christmas, likely my father's last, would be no exception.

Christmas Eve was a night of work. Everything for Christmas dinner was to be prepared in advance, with the dishes set out on the dining room table, the silver and crystal polished, and the napkins ironed and folded. In the morning, there would be no presents from Santa until breakfast was eaten and the dishes washed. Then—and only then—could anyone enter the living room, where the color-coordinated tree sat, looking quite forlorn and underdressed. It was the same tree, with the same decorations and the same few strands of recycled tinsel, that we'd used since I was little.

My daughter had never known any Christmas like it, and it broke my heart to have to tell her to wait, wait, and wait before she could enjoy her Christmas morning. But finally, the last of the dishes were dried and put away, and my mother instructed us to be seated at the tree.

We all sat on the floor, where my father would hand out the presents one at a time. Only one person at a time could unwrap his or her gift, and the paper wasn't to be torn. Each present had to be opened carefully so that the paper didn't tear, and before the opener could admire the gift, the paper had to be handed to my mother, who would press it out, fold it neatly, and lay it into a pile to be used the following year. Proper comments were followed by proper "thank yous," with a pause between people opening gifts as my mother would question the recipient on what he or she really thought of the gift, as if the first words were lies and the "thank yous" insufficient. The slightest deviation from the expected tone or expression of gratitude was met with a firm rebuke from my mother and a threat that there'd be no future gift giving if the gift giver wasn't properly appreciated. Unless, of course, I was the gift giver, in which case the rules were upside down. Whatever I gave was inevitably the wrong thing, and I was immediately scolded for not having the sense to give a more appropriate gift. And so it always went.

Only when my mother was satisfied with the response to a gift could my father pass the next gift to the next person for the same tedious routine.

Opened in this manner, Christmas presents didn't feel like gifts at all but instead like ticking time bombs, each one having the capacity to make our family explode at any moment.

Usually, I received nothing more than a practical pair of white support hose or something equally absurd, like tea towels from my mother's church bazaar or writing paper or pens. But this year, there was something out of the ordinary. It was a large box, very long, almost like what would have held a Christmas tree. And it had my name on it. She would glance at it often and smile, but something about it made me shiver. It looked almost like a coffin.

Finally, the gifts were all opened, except for the box. As my father passed it to me, she started telling a story about being up in the "barn." That's what we called the garage because at one time it had been an old carriage house, and she had been up there looking through all our old things. I was never allowed up there; if I tried to go in there to look for anything, she would follow me out there and question what I was doing or what I was looking for, so eventually, I just stayed away.

"And while I was up there," she went on, "I could hear these babies crying for their mommy. So I dug through all that old stuff until I found them all. And those babies were so cold and dirty, and not dressed properly at all, so I brought them into the house."

By this point, my daughter was looking frightened as her grandma talked about babies in the garage crying for their mommy, and I was totally creeped out. But she wasn't done.

"So I gave them all baths and spent a great deal of time making clothes for them. I just hope you appreciate all that I did for your babies."

I really had no idea what she was talking about. But my dad apparently did, though he just sighed heavily, clearly anxious to get outside for a smoke.

"Mommy, can I go outside and play?" my little girl asked, getting restless.

"Not until everyone has opened their presents," my mother sternly told her.

I gave her an assuring look and then slowly started to open my creepy gift. Inside were several old dolls placed toe to toe, covered up with their arms over the blankets, looking as if they were, indeed, lying in a coffin. I was horrified.

I had no words. No words at all. What I had wanted from that "barn" of an attic was my music, my writing, my world from Hazelton that she had, years before, cleared out when I was in the hospital. She had tossed that whole world out, and I had hoped, somehow, that my "babies" inside that box would be my songs. Not these creepy dolls I'd never even played with.

I knew in that moment, as I gazed down at that box of babies, that things were going to be changing very quickly. Her slips into another world would be more frequent. She was unable to deal with the fact that her husband was dying and she would be left all alone.

I stared into that box and asked myself if I could be there for her.

And I knew that I couldn't. I knew that I might be there in person, might cook and clean for her and nurse her as she aged, but I knew that I could never bring myself to feel love for the woman who'd treated those plastic dolls with more loving care than she'd ever treated me.

It was our last Christmas together in that house as a family. As my dad grew weaker, his life was soon reduced to continual trips to the toilet. The tumors had filled his bladder, and he had to urinate almost constantly. Although he'd had surgeries to remove them, they always grew back, and by the following fall, they removed what was left of a useless bladder full of cancer. The surgery should have been done much sooner, and if it had, he might have lived. I never got an answer for why they had waited so long—whether it was because of the doctors or my father himself. All I knew was by the time they removed his bladder, the cancer had spread throughout his body.

The trip to the hospital was forty-five minutes each way, but I made it daily after school to keep him company, bathe him, and comfort him while my mother stayed home. She acted as if my father had just gone away for a few days and would be back soon; she visited him only when the weather was clear and warm. She didn't seem to grasp that he was dying, or if she did, she didn't show it. She stayed focused on the house and her social life, just as if nothing unusual was happening.

As soon as my father was stable enough, he was transferred to a hospital in Belleville, and then soon after, he came home. But that didn't last long; within days, he worsened and had to be readmitted to the hospital, where he spent his last days on earth. Every day, I would take him down the hall for a smoke, and it was during those moments that I would try to get him to talk about his death arrangements. When I explained to him about a DNR order—a directive to the physician and nursing staff not to resuscitate him if his heart stopped—he would have no part of it. He wasn't ready to die, even though his body clearly was.

But to me, my father had left quite some time before. It was as if his spirit had drained along with the blood that passed through him, the blood-red jars of pee like some ghoulish trophy that Death had been awarded.

Finally, in February of 1987, my father's fight to stay alive came to an end.

My mother had made no preparations. Taking her to the funeral home was a nightmare. She almost climbed inside one of the displays, determined to be sure my father would be comfortable in his casket. Relatives I hadn't seen for decades crawled out of the woodwork, only a few acknowledging my daughter or me. It was as if we weren't even there. She had told everyone years ago that I was dead, and although I was physically present, I had been buried along with my past.

We kept to ourselves upstairs; my mother lived in her own world underneath us. Occasionally, I'd hear loud voices and screeches that belonged to someone I didn't know. It was as if my father's death had given my mother's psyche permission to let loose, unrestrained. I was close to graduation and I spent most of my time at the hospital, leaving my daughter with my mother after school.

One night, shortly after my father was buried, I came home from work and found my mother and daughter sitting at the table, set for four. My little girl was dressed in an old, pink dress that my mother had made for me when I was a few years younger than her.

I stood, mesmerized by what I saw before me.

"Claire!" my mother screeched to my daughter. "You answer your father right now!!" My daughter looked up at me, her blue eyes streaming with tears.

"What the hell do you think you're doing?" I screamed as I grabbed my daughter's small arm and yanked her out of the chair.

"Who are you?" my mother asked me, as if I were a total stranger. "You don't belong here! Get out! Get out! Get out!" She picked up a plate and hurled it at me, missing me by inches. It smashed against the wall and an explosion of porcelain fragments flew through the air. Just as she reached for another, I pushed my little girl out the door and we both took the stairs two at a time. We locked ourselves in our apartment and listened to the sounds of more smashing porcelain.

With one arm, I hugged my daughter, and with the other, I reached for the phone. I called my uncle, my mother's youngest brother.

"I think you'd better come visit," I said and relayed what had just happened. "She needs more help than I can provide."

"It's an hour's drive, so it's getting too late to come down tonight, but I'll be there in the morning."

"I'll be at work then, but just come on in and check on her. I'll plan on coming back for lunch."

We hung up, and I felt relieved to know that something was going to be done about my mother. Once her brother saw how delusional she'd become, he'd help me get her into a safer place before something really bad, like a fire or her wandering off, could happen.

When I pulled into the driveway the next afternoon, there was my uncle's car. My body lightened with the relief of passing over her care to her *real* family—which she had always made clear did not include me.

I went straight up to our apartment and began to do some paperwork, confident that whatever was going on downstairs was between the siblings and when my uncle was ready, he'd come up and let me know what was going on.

And sure enough, I heard his heavy footsteps on the stairs coming closer, and then a sharp rapping on the door. I opened it, and the first thing I saw where his eyes, like poison darts, staring straight into mine.

"Listen," he hissed, "you have to stop doing this!" I was stunned by his anger.

"Doing what?" I replied. "I didn't do anything! What did she tell you?"

"Stop making these wild accusations. It's all such nonsense, total nonsense. I don't have time to drive down here every time you and your mother have a fight!"

"But we didn't have a fight—she thought my daughter was me, and she was screaming at her to listen to my dead father!"

"Can't you just leave her alone?" he replied. "She's grieving. Now, don't call me again!"

I stared back at him in shock. I couldn't think of a word to say, I was so confused.

"She was fine," he continued. "She was all dressed up, with her makeup on. She had lunch ready. She was pleasant and appropriate. She says that you're the one that needs the help, and quite frankly, I agree." He turned abruptly and stormed down the stairs and out the door, leaving me shell-shocked.

It was clearly time for us to move out of that house of horrors. I'd be graduating soon, and there was no better time to start our life anew, away from my mother.

My adoptive parents

Trained to perform at an early age

Mother and me, note the clenched fist

The perfect family

Me, age 5yrs in Metz France wearing the famous dress

Me, age 19yrs

Me when we lived with Shelly

Me and my gang. Metz France

Graduation, a new chapter begins

Someone I loved once gave me a box full of darkness.
It took me years to understand that this, too, was a gift.
—Mary Oliver

Chapter 11

A Little too Late

When I graduated with first-class honors, my pride was dampened by my secret shame. I felt as if I was somehow a fraud, as if I'd be found out at any minute to be unworthy of my achievements. A part of me was missing, and in its place was a tiny part that wanted to scream at that anonymous woman on the telephone who told me I could never be a nurse, to scream at everyone who had never expected anything of me, who had written me off as undeserving or dead. Instead of feeling victorious because I had proven them wrong, I felt only furious. And I had no idea where that fury was coming from, other than deep down inside me.

But I knew better than to let people see the pain I was feeling. I stored my pain in my Wall of Secrets, and I walked across the stage to receive my diploma—and with it, my new identity as a college graduate and nurse—with my head held high and a smile on my face.

Each day after, as I climbed into my white uniform and ever so carefully took my cap with its prized double-black stripes from its protective plastic housing, I pinned it to my hair with pride and disbelief. I could not believe that I'd really earned those stripes that distinguished me as a registered nurse. It was a lifetime ago that I had donned a white lab coat and wandered around the hospital with my friend Daryl, pretending I was hospital staff. Now I no longer had to pretend; I was the real thing, even if deep down inside, I didn't quite believe it.

I chose this chapter in my nursing career to be in acute-care psychiatry. How ironic and yet purposeful that I would find myself caring for the very same people I once was—broken and damaged, addicted and angry. Of course, I was still filled with sadness, but I no longer turned the rage of pain against myself. Instead, I did my best to focus my anger on my survival. If I were to succeed in this new life and career, the battle I would wage would be a battle against pain, in all its many forms. And as I realized that, I saw how fitting it was that I would start my career on the psychiatric ward. My own life experiences had brought me to a place where I could help others who were suffering as I once did. I could understand madness and addiction, because I had lived so close to it and at times, right inside of it.

But why I still felt so fundamentally different—from both those I cared for and those I lived and worked among—perplexed me. Why was it that I felt I did not belong in any world, whatever world I ventured into? Why was it that I felt so constantly excluded, as if I were allowed to peer through the windows of these other worlds always on the outside, but never step through their doors to claim my place in the world? Why did I so fear a real connection to anybody else? What had made me like this?

But I was connected to my daughter. No matter what happened, I would not lose that connection, nor did I fear that I would. No one and nothing could take away my child. She was becoming a beautiful testament to what life can and should be. She was strong and secure with a heart full of love, joy, and trust. She was all of the things I never had nor could find as an adult.

We had rented a little house a few blocks away from my mother. I couldn't bear to live with her a moment longer, yet I could not bring myself to leave her all alone. As my new identity as a nurse slowly became reality and I accepted my new role, I could not simply abandon my mother. If I could not care for her as a daughter, I could at least care for her as a nurse. I knew she needed someone to take care of her, even if she had never really cared for me. Maybe somehow, some way, we could find peace between us before she died.

But caring for her was exasperating. She berated me constantly for my flaws and imperfections and constantly reminded me that whatever it was that I was or was not doing to help her was wrong. She still told me I should be dead, that I deserved all the blows in my life but none of my achievements. It was as if I kept going back for some sudden proof that she did love me, when I left each afternoon knowing she did not. I was beating my head against the wall in my efforts to please my mother, even though it was an impossible task. Caring for her made going to work all the more rewarding—it was far better to care for a whole ward of mentally ill people than just that one.

Or so I thought. I was working the night shift one night as charge nurse. It was a usual shift, nothing out of the ordinary, except for one thing: a patient who had been under twenty-four-hour observation in the intensive treatment area had been sent back to our floor by the staff physician just before I came on.

The patient, Dale, was a tall, good-looking guy with clever wit and a gentle soul. Dale was one of my favorites, but he had been suffering from pretty severe depression in recent weeks, and he just didn't seem ready to come out to the ward so soon. I wasn't alone in my assessment; the whole nursing staff agreed that it was a bad decision, and something bad might well come of it. So with that news to start my shift, the air was alive with nervous tension.

I'd spent enough time living on the streets of Toronto, in jail, and with motorcycle gangs, as well in my mother's home, to know that when I had a bad feeling about something, it was usually for a reason. Like everyone on shift that night, I had a bad feeling, but as charge nurse, I had to present an image of confidence and control. So I put on my poker face, pushed the worries from my head, and focused on getting through report. After report was over, it was time for my rounds.

I went from room to room checking on patients, flashlight in hand, standing beside each bed watching chests rise and fall and quietly questioning those awake in regards to medications or reasons they were awake. All was in order, until I reached Dale's room, where a chill overcame me and for a split second, I froze. But I dismissed my fears, pushed through clouds of uncertainty, and walked right in, only to find his bed empty. I knocked on the bathroom door, but there was no answer, so I opened it.

I'll never forget what I saw. Dale was hanging from a long, leather tie he'd tied into a noose and hung from the ceiling grate, his face ghastly pale and his tongue swollen and protruding from his mouth. He was probably dead, I knew, but there was still a chance.

I rushed to him and hoisted his body up as much as I could to relieve the pressure, then shouted, "Code Blue!" He was incredibly heavy, and just pushing him a few inches was more than I could bear.

"Help me!" I shouted again, and a clamor on the ward erupted in excitement. His best friend, from the next room, rushed in and grabbed hold of his legs and hoisted him up. I grabbed a chair and frantically cut the leather ties from around his neck, the weight of his lifeless body nearly toppling the schizophrenic friend. When we got him onto the floor, I started CPR just as the orderlies and cardiac-arrest team arrived.

But it was too late. Dale was already dead.

I stayed home from work for the next couple of days; the memories of finding Dale's body played over and over inside my head like a constant film reel. I couldn't sleep and could barely eat. When I'd worked in Toronto, if there was ever a suicide, a psychiatric team was on the spot for a debriefing within the hour to help us to cope with the trauma we'd witnessed. But there was nothing at this hospital, no debriefing, no discussion, nothing at all, not even a lousy pamphlet with a number we could call for help. No one even asked how I was, and as the thoughts and memories of that moment entered my nightmares, as much as my waking hours, I became furious that Dale had died so unnecessarily and that I was suffering from the trauma unnecessarily. I felt utterly helpless to control my thoughts, just as Dale, too, must have felt utterly helpless to control his own destructive thoughts.

For months, that night was frozen in my mind, and when another patient killed himself shortly after, all the anguish came barreling down on me all over again. I couldn't stop reliving those minutes when I burst into Dale's room and saw his lifeless body hanging, his face swollen into something indescribably inhuman and macabre. I couldn't stop the tears that burst from me at the most unexpected moments. Finally, I knew I had to see a doctor. I wouldn't be able to continue in my job if moments like that became so wounding.

I began seeing a psychiatrist, Dr. Finster, a funny little guy who dressed in sloppy suits and had a head shaped like an egg. It was bald on top, with a shaggy fringe of hair that gave him a clownish air.

He wasn't exactly warm and fuzzy; he was more cold and clinical, detached and unsmiling. On the rare occasions when he would smile, it was a slanted smile, like he couldn't quite commit to it.

Yet I liked him. Our sessions gave me a space to talk about things I'd kept tucked away for years, a place where I felt safe and if I was judged, at least I was judged dispassionately.

Dr. Finster was less interested in focusing on the trauma than he was on the first sixteen years of my life, before I'd left home. He wanted to know all about my mother and our relationship, and he was fascinated by the smallest details. Any effort I made to discuss the hanging was quickly dismissed as linked in some inexplicable way to my relationship with my mother. I finally decided that there was little point in expecting him to help me recover from the trauma, but I could at least use the opportunity to better understand the isolation and torment that my life had come to be.

While I told him of the abuse I suffered as a child, I was struck by the irony of the abuse I was continuing to endure as an adult. Since I had left my mother's home, our relationship continued to deteriorate, but I did my best to take care of her. Still, it was a challenge because I couldn't seem to do anything to please her.

"What took you so long? That's not the kind I like; you're always buying the wrong thing. When are you going to take me shopping? I can't eat this. I don't want that." On and on it went, until I got to the point where I hated taking care of her. But still I did, still bound and determined to gain her love, ever the grateful and obligated adoptee.

"Why do you keep going back there?" Dr. Finster asked. It wasn't a rhetorical question; he really wanted me to think through the answer.

"Because I have to."

"No, you don't."

"Well, then, who will?"

"You said she has family, friends. If she is abusing you, then you are under no obligation to return. But you do. What is it that you want from her?"

"I guess I want her to tell me she loves me. I want her to love me before she dies."

"And has she shown any indication that she is going to do that?"

"No."

"But still you go back."

"Yes."

I felt almost ashamed that I was taking care of her, but I just couldn't bring myself to abandon her. I knew what it was like to be abandoned. At least once a day, I drove down the long, winding road to my mother's house, and as soon as I would turn into her driveway, the familiar sensations of impending doom would flood my body and soul. My face flushed and the heat shot sparks from my scalps, as if an electrical current had struck me. My belly tied itself into knots as I walked toward the door to the house I grew up in, and I was filled with trepidation every time.

I told myself that I was in training, training to be stronger and braver. I told myself each time I walked toward my childhood home that I was only practicing for greater challenges, desensitizing myself to pain. If I could master my pain and fear without panicking, I told myself, I could deal with any assault she hurled at me. The driveway was a trial by ordeal, a trial I had to master each day as I trained myself to be a warrior caregiver, a woman who could handle any patient, no matter how cruel.

The only way I could deal with my mother was by categorizing her as another psychiatric patient.

I ran errands for her, checked in on her, and watched as her mind and health rapidly declined. As I battled to endure a mother's hatred, a lifetime of hatred stuffed down my throat with every word she spoke to me, I learned to stuff my own rage and pain into a drawer in my Wall of Secrets. Even though The Wall itself had disappeared, the secrets it contained had not. They lived on.

Old wounds left untreated do not heal. I searched inside my mother's fading eyes for the compassion I needed to care for her in her decline, but all I could discern was a pained woman. A sad and bitter woman who did not experience her own spirit being nurtured and so could not nurture another. But it was no excuse for her abuse and neglect of me as a child, and it was no excuse for her abuse of me as I cared for her in her final years.

My career advanced, my daughter grew, and my mother became sicker and less aware. Years passed, and still I cared for her every day. Finally, in the spring of 2000, my mother's decline had become evident. She was no longer able to stay alone in the large home she had lived in for most of her long life. She was afraid of parting from her possessions.

"You just want to get me out of here so you can have my things!" she spat when I raised the issue of moving to an extended-care facility.

"No, Mother, I don't want your things," I assured her, "but you need more care than I can give you."

"I'm perfectly fine here. I just need some extra help. Why don't you send a girl in to help me out? I'll tell you why—because you can't wait to get your hands on my estate!"

Her "estate" had declined over the years until all that was left was a big, old house that had been neglected for years and would take far more money to restore than it was worth. The lake properties had been sold years before, and my mother had stored the proceeds somewhere like a squirrel stores its winter stash to see it through until spring. There was nothing but a lot of old furniture and china, hardly enough to cover her expenses. But in her mind, she was a wealthy woman surrounded by greedy relatives who cared only for her "things."

By the end of the year, my mother died—finally, eternally, letting go of her "things."

Her last words to me were, "I love you."

But it was too late. My own love for her had died years before.

After the funeral, I was cleaning out her house to ready it for sale, when I came upon a box underneath her bed. I opened it, and inside were dozens of bank ledgers, tied together in neat little bundles, each with a year marking them.

I pulled one out, and as I read, my hands began to shake and huge droplets fell from my eyes onto the pages.

She had written down every cent she'd ever spent on me, all the way back to the week I was adopted.

The cost of a two-cent bow, the nickel for ice cream, the cost of my share of the groceries as a child, the cost of a fifty-cent toy— anything and everything that had a price tag, she had documented.

She had tallied the cost of my existence, up until the day she died.

And left it for me to find, one final slap in the face after she was buried in her grave. I had been bought and paid for and in return had been expected to perform a certain job.

Let us go forth, the tellers of talks,
And seize whatever prey the heart long for
And have no fear. Everything exists, everything is true
And the earth is only a little dust under our feet.
—W.B. Yeats

Chapter 12

Can it Be Real?

I stood there, staring up at it. Above the clothes, on the shelf, there it was. My old, tarnished tin box that had sat in my closet since I'd moved back to Belleville, taken down a couple of times each year for yet another close inspection. Inside was my true identity, written on tattered paper. I knew when I took off the lid, my tear ducts would open and all the pent-up emotion inside me could no longer be held back. On those rare occasions when I did open it, hoping that something might be revealed, something new might be discovered, I closed it with disappointment. Nothing inside it ever changed. There was never anything new to be revealed, just a name on a tattered piece of paper. A tattered name, a tattered identity. My true self.

Inside the box was also the number I had called years before, when the woman who answered told me her aunt could be my mother, only to find that phone number disconnected one week later. That disconnected number was the closest link I had to someone who might possibly be my mother. Scribbled on that same scrap of paper was a name—my name, the name that was taken away from me when I was given away. I had no name.

I held the box in my lap; my hands trembled. Years before, I had read a magazine article about adoption laws changing and it gave me a small speck of hope, just enough to make my hands tremble every time I held the old, tin box that contained my true self. The article had listed options for adoptees to find their birth parents, and it included a phone number for the Alberta Adoption Registry in Alberta, my birthplace. I had sent them a request to be registered with them and if someone wanted to find me and contacted them, they could put us in touch. It was a long shot, but it was the only shot I had. If my birth mother wanted to find me, and if she set out to find me, and if she knew about this agency, and if she contacted this agency, then we could find each other. It seemed nearly impossible, if not implausible, that it could actually work, but I knew only one thing: if I didn't contact them, there was no possibility at all that she could find me if she were, indeed, looking for me. Adoption records had been sealed up until now. This was my chance. Surely, she would want to find me, knowing I had been looking since I found that cousin years ago.

So every year, I called them on my birthday, knowing, of course, if anyone had been trying to find me, they would have called *me*. And every year, the answer was the same: "No, I'm sorry, but we don't have anything. Don't give up hope."

And every year, I hung up the phone and let the tears fall down my face.

It was my fiftieth birthday. A year I should have been celebrating, but instead, just as every year, I was home, alone, surrounded by silence and memories. And like every year, I picked up the telephone and dialed the number to the agency.

And like every year, I was told that no one was looking for me.

Was she even alive? If she was, I knew it wouldn't be for long. Even if she'd been a teenager when I was born, she would be advancing in age. If I was ever going to find my birth mother, I had to come up with a different plan.

I decided to hire a private detective. I began doing some research and discovered that with the loosening of the adoption laws, there were actual search agencies that helped people who'd been adopted or put their children up for adoption to locate their parents and children. With a small sum I'd inherited from my mother, I hired an agency and gave them what limited information I had.

For months, nothing happened. Then one day, I got a phone call.

"Sit down," said the voice on the other end of the phone. "I have something important to tell you." I was stunned, and after snatching up a pen and paper, I slowly lowered myself into a chair. The seconds that passed felt endless, as a million thoughts whizzed around in my head.

"You are not going to believe it," the woman said, the excitement in her voice palpable.

"Wh … what is it? Have you found my birth mother? Who is she? Is she still living? Where does she live? Is she looking for me?"

"Your birth mother is alive, and you have two sisters and a brother," she said, as the words hung in the air and in my ears. She was right. I couldn't believe it.

"My birth mother? Two sisters? And a brother?" I echoed back, afraid I hadn't heard right and in an instant the moment would be snatched away and I'd hear an apology and dial tone, as I had so many times before.

"Yes, a family!" she squealed in delight.

"Who? Where? Do they know?" I realized I was shouting into the phone, I was so excited.

"You can only have their names and ages for now," she said. "They all have to agree to contact first."

Somehow, that didn't seem right. I was part of their family, and they had to give me permission? They held my medical history, my heritage, proof of my existence. Her words were like a foreign language to me. My brain was unable to make sense of them properly, but somehow, the conversation ended and there I was, alone with a list of names written on a piece of paper. *Carol. Laura. Jim.* Most importantly: *Marilyn*, my mother.

I wandered the floor most of the night with that piece of paper held before me and repeated their names over and over. Did I finally belong somewhere? Was this *my* family? A few weeks later, on the day after Valentine's Day 2003, the phone rang again, and I had my answer.

"Hello? Hello? Is this Claire?" A strange voice asked me, slightly hesitant.

"Yes ..." I answered, equally hesitant. "Who is this?"

"This is Carol. Your sister."

For a moment, I was stunned into silence, unable to formulate the letters of the word *sister* into anything comprehensible. I had never had a sister; it was a completely alien concept.

"Oh, my God," I sputtered. "How are you?" I immediately regretted the question; it seemed so inappropriate for the situation, as if my sister were someone I actually knew. My hands were shaking, and the conversation that came out of my mouth played out in a staccato format.

She told me about her family. I told her about mine.

"Do you want to speak to your mother?" she asked. I was terrified and excited at the same time, not sure how to respond.

"Sure, of course I do." I squeezed the words into the phone between my tears, and then, in an instant, a new voice came through the phone and into my ear.

"Hello … this is your mother," the voice said. Like an electric current had shot through me, I stiffened with chills. Any words I had planned to say were stuck in my brain, unable to be pulled out.

Again, I asked, "How are you?" I was in shock. I had no words. She had no words. More than half a century had passed between us, a century between the two of us, something words could not make sense of, something words could not undo.

Promises were made to speak again soon, and before I knew it, the phone was returned to its cradle and I was standing in the same spot I'd been standing in just minutes before, but I'd become an entirely different person.

I was someone. I was Marilyn's daughter. I was Carol's sister. My life had changed forever.

"Your nose," Carol said, in our next conversation.

"What about my nose?" I asked.

"What does it look like? Do you have a bump? Is it big?" She was chuckling, not interrogating. She was happy to speak with me, curious herself to learn of me and know me.

"I sure do," I said. "And I hate it!"

"Good!" Carol laughed. "We would have been pretty upset if you were the only one to get a good nose!"

The idea that I might actually look like someone, a real person, that someone other than my daughter was genetically similar to me, was overwhelming. No one had ever looked like me before. No one had ever shared my hated nose, the nose that stuck out of my face like a beacon to tell the world I wasn't a real Hitchon. No Hitchon had such a nose.

I suddenly loved my nose.

"If you want to see her, you should come soon," Carol said in another telephone conversation. "Our mother is very ill. She has emphysema and lung cancer. We don't know how long she will make it. It could be a few more years or maybe a few more months. We don't know. It's good that you found us when you did."

We had only spoken a few times, but already, I felt transformed.

When I hung up the phone, I called my daughter and told her we were going to Vancouver Island.

At 7:55 a.m., I sunk into the backseat of a taxi, already in tears. I was headed to the train to go to Toronto where I'd meet my daughter, who was away at university.

The train ride was a roller coaster from hell. As the train jostled and rocked along the tracks, I tried to sip from my coffee without spilling it, my train ticket gripped tightly in my hand. The noises surrounding me grew louder as voices tried to outdo the others in pitch. Some sort of teacher's group, I imagined. They were talking with great animation for such an early hour as they discussed their kids, classroom kids, home kids, and everyone's kids.

It was an ordinary day to these travelers, but an extraordinary day for me. I was embarking on the most important journey of my life, but I didn't feel thrilled. I felt shocked. I wanted to scream at the train to stop making so much noise, to listen to my soul screaming in confusion. Where was I going? Who was I going to meet? What were the stories I'd be told?

I had no idea. I was going to a home that had never been my home, to a mother who had never been my mother, to learn the stories of this family's past, a past that had never been my past. I didn't know what to make of it. I wanted to scream, "I'm another kind of kid!"

A kind they probably didn't even know existed.

I tuned into the conversation across the aisle. They were talking about security, but they weren't being very secure. I could hear every word.

My ears shifted from one conversation to another, as the conversation in my own head grew louder than them all.

"We have no idea how she'll react," Carol had told me.

I wanted my mother to wrap me in her arms and tell me how much she loved me. How she thought of me every day and searched desperately to find me. I wanted her to say she was sorry and hold me close while our genetic markers at long last reconnected. I wanted to crawl back inside her womb and curl up and go to sleep for nine long months and re-emerge reborn and renewed, cradled by my mother.

But I knew that was asking a lot from a stranger who gave me away and never looked back.

Or did she? Did she look back? Did she regret her decision to give me to somebody else to raise? Did she even know how I was raised? Did she think I had "a good home," with material comforts and love? My parents had spun a web of deception around my arrival. Did she do the same about my disappearance?

Huge, huge holes of sadness filled with grief as the train jiggled and rocked. A grief so intense I didn't think I could survive it began rising from my belly to my throat. I wanted to roar out in pain.

By the time I got to my daughter, I was a mess.

"Mom, it's going to be fine; there's no reason to cry," she told me as soon as she took one look at me. Although her words were comforting, I could sense the exasperation in her voice and my own anger rising in response, but I pushed it back down. How could she possibly understand? She couldn't understand what such a moment meant for me, because she'd always had me. She had no reference point, no idea what it was like to be given away at birth, unwanted and rejected.

She squeezed my hand. "I know," she said. "It's like meeting my dad."

Of course she had a reference point; how could I have forgotten? For years, I had sent Mike, her father, photos of her and letters to tell him how she was doing, but he would just ignore them or once in awhile write back to tell me not to contact him ever again. He had returned to his wife and family and didn't consider her part of that family.

She had me and knew she was wanted and loved. Somehow, it felt so much more painful to be abandoned by a mother.

A cab was called to take us to the airport, and when it arrived, she had to practically stuff me into the backseat; I was so reluctant to move. As thrilled as I was to be meeting my mother, a part of me was terrified—a very big part of me.

I lit a cigarette and sucked it down as I blew the smoke out the windows of the cab. I couldn't even remember when I'd taken up the habit, but every effort I made to quit went nowhere.

"Damn these smokes," I said as I flicked the last of the cigarette out the window.

My daughter glared. She hated me smoking.

I felt like a masochist, piling the stress onto myself until I cracked, and then adding some more, as if to bury myself in it.

We were making the trip together, yet I knew the journey was mine and mine alone. The adventure belonged to us both, but the internal torment belonged only to me.

After fifty years of emptiness, there was finally a glimmer of hope that I would find something to fill that dark place inside me that festered like an infected wound and tainted every day of my life, revealing hideous, painful secrets to be shoved away in my Wall.

Now the drawers to The Wall were opening, and my secrets were being revealed.

The secret of my birth, the secret that shadowed my life.

There had been so much pain in my life, such trauma, such loss, that to even think for a second that it might change was surreal and unbelievable. I felt as if I were having an out-of-body experience and all that was happening was happening to another person, someone who looked like me but wasn't me. I reached up to touch my face and felt the warm and wet tears that proved otherwise. It was really me, the real—but secret—me. The one that had been given away and was now, at long last, returning, if not to the womb, to the wound.

I was going home to my mother.

My real mother.

What would she do when she saw me? Would she just sit there like a statue and stare? Would my sisters and my brother do the same? Would they surround me and look at me like I was some sort of invader from outer space?

I could handle that. Since I had expected never to find them, certainly never to meet them, I had expected nothing. To stare at me would be so much more than nothing, that I could accept it if that was how they met me.

And I would be staring back. I would stare at each of them, searching for myself.

When there are secrets in a family, there is a conspiracy of silence. It's a nonverbal one, but it is there, nonetheless. It holds the family members together in a negative energy force, while at the same time keeping them apart. Secrets are like warm blankets you hide under with a friend, only they smother you, make you sick. My understanding so far was that this family carried many secrets, for many years. The fact that they had a sister was known to others but not to my siblings.

Would we heal together as a family? Would we all recognize our wounds from having a family member torn away? Would we grow strong and heal together?

I was terrified.

The silver-winged bird slid into a new world, pushing me into the pale-blue striped velour seat of the airplane. I forced my body to become part of the velour; the light-gray plastic arms of the seatbelt wrapped around my waist and held me in place as the plane sped along the runway toward the waiting gate. We'd landed in Victoria on Vancouver Island, British Columbia.

I looked around and marveled at the distant greenery and blurred colors of blooming flowers, marking a springtime that hadn't yet arrived in Ontario, where the snow was still piled high. It was fitting that the cold, white landscape of winter should be gone for this new journey of my life, replaced by newborn life exploding into the world with a burst of color.

I couldn't hold back my emotions any longer; they swelled from my belly and choked off any rational thought I might have had. Moving my head slightly to the right, I stared at my grown daughter. Her nose was pressed into the glass as she watched the scenery pass as we came to a stop. It was a new world to her as well, I realized. She was about to meet an unknown family. Aunts she never knew existed. A grandmother. There was no fear in her eyes, only excitement for the new adventure on the horizon.

My own eyes held enough terror for the both of us. Although my mother wouldn't be meeting me at the airport because her emphysema kept her pretty much confined to home, I would be meeting my sister and brother any minute. That was actually better. It would give me time to adjust, to ready myself for the big meeting.

I poked her in the side with a jab of my elbow, trying to get her attention.

"What, Mom?" she asked, reluctantly moving her eyes from the window to stare into mine. Whatever it was she saw in them, it seemed to unsettle her. "What's the matter? Aren't you excited? Why are you crying?"

"I don't know," I answered, our caregiver roles reversed. Now I was the one in need of support, and she the one who provided it. "I'm so scared."

"It'll be okay; don't worry," she said, reassuring me before she turned her head back to the scenery.

I didn't believe her. How could everything possibly be okay? My eyes focused on the white paper draped over the headrest of the man in the seat in front of me. It flapped like a sheet in the wind as the silver bird grinded to a stop. This was it. My new life was about to begin.

If tears were pearls, I would have become a rich woman that day. They fell rapidly, strand upon strand decorating my new reunion shirt. Passengers on both sides of the aisle chattered like excited squirrels as they opened the overhead compartments that held their memories of home or vacation adventures. I sat, paralyzed. My hands were wrapped around the gray plastic armrests; I squeezed them so tight, I expected them to shatter. My knuckles were blanched as white as the paper sheet on the headrest in front of me; it had stopped fluttering and now lay motionless, a blank screen I patiently stared at as I waited for my future to start playing.

I turned to look at my daughter and saw that she had already unbuckled her seatbelt and anxiously waited for me to do the same. My eyes searched her face, as if wanting to memorize her features one last time before encountering my new family, just to be sure of our genetic connection. Her eyes sparkled with blue-water diamonds that betrayed her excitement; some days, her eyes were hazel and spoke the same language as my own brown eyes. But this day, they were cool and clear and glowed with her building enthusiasm to meet our ancestral bloodline. Her creamy-colored complexion was accented with two roses blooming on her cheeks. I could see the anticipation building inside her. Tiny tendrils of reddish curls had escaped their twisted homes and framed her face, which reminded me of the small and innocent child she once was. As her excitement blossomed, so, too, did my fear, until it had grown from a pulsing anxiety to a full-force terror.

I felt the air being sucked from me, as if my entire body was collapsing into itself, becoming smaller and smaller until I would disappear. My eyes felt as if a red-hot poker were piercing them from the inside out until they bulged from their sockets. I wondered if anyone could tell, if my burning, bulging, terrified eyes were visible to the rest of the world, or if I had somehow concealed them from public view. The burning sensation spread upward to my scalp until it felt as if my hair would burst into flames at any moment.

Trickles of sweat scampered down my sides like tears springing from my armpits. My whole body was crying.

"I can't ... I just can't." I exhaled the words and hoped she would understand and somehow save me from the approaching reunion. If we could just stay on the plane and follow it to its next stop, I would be all right.

"What do you mean, you can't? You can't what?" she asked, confused.

"Can't get off," I said. "I can't leave this plane."

"Mom, you have to get off the plane. You can't stay here," she said, clearly becoming annoyed.

I glared back at her. I understood her; why couldn't she understand me? I realized she had accompanied me only on the external journey, not the internal one. She couldn't possibly understand the emotional avalanche inside me that was taking over my rational being.

I watched from the corner of my eye as she fidgeted, pulled her burgundy sweater sleeves down around her fists, and stared back at me, her head tilted as if looking into my soul for an understandable explanation.

A quiet hush had filled the space where the other passengers had sat only minutes before. She stood, bent at the waist, in the closed space of the seats as she nudged me with her knee to get up and let her out.

"Unbuckle, Mom," she ordered.

I sighed deeply and tried to release my fear, as I released my tenacious grip on the armrests and did as she instructed. My arms immediately wrapped themselves around me and held me in a tight hug, as if to hold me back, to keep me safe inside the plane.

"Mom, get up! You have to move. Everyone has left the plane. You're going to get us in trouble." Her annoyance had turned to anger, and I knew she was right. But why couldn't she know that I was right, too?

"Okay, okay," I said, "just give me a second. Don't rush me." I spit out the words, matching her anger with my own.

"Rush you?" she shot back. "Good grief, we're the last ones here. Move!"

I inhaled deeply, hoping to find oxygen in the stale air, but there was none. Instead, I breathed in a cloud of anxiety and dread that settled and rolled in my belly, until I felt nauseous with bile about to erupt from my throat.

I covered my mouth with a Kleenex, just in case. There was no sense in embarrassing my daughter any more than I already had. I rocked back and forth in my seat and tried to comfort myself as I rested my sweat-covered forehead against the seat in front of me.

"It's okay; it's okay; it's okay," I whispered to myself.

You can do this, Claire. You can do this. You can do this.

The rapidly spoken words made me breathless, and I began to hyperventilate. I had to get off the plane, get some air, real air. I wrapped my fingers around the armrests again and pushed myself up, wishing the plastic arms would pull me back down and not let me go. As I did so, I noticed the flight attendant standing in the aisle a few seats away, watching me from a distance.

"Is there a problem?" she asked, her mouth fixed in a smile but her eyes expressing their disapproval.

"No," my angry daughter answered, "we're leaving now." She glared at me and pushed me sideways into the aisle. I brushed off the wrinkles I had accumulated on my clothes and stretched to make sure I could stand. My knees threatened to buckle from the stress and demands to make my legs move. My internal conversation had taken over once again. I tried to capture my daughter's words and pull them into my ears, but they didn't want to hear. She was instructing me to move. She had passed me my backpack and was propelling me forward. Reluctantly, I moved one foot ahead and pulled the other behind; I made slow progress up the aisle. Everything felt too tight: the plane, my clothes, and my flesh. I felt my shoes strangling my toes, my jeans holding the air inside my belly, suffocating me. My jacket pulled my shoulders back, when all they wanted to do was hunch over. Everything was uncomfortable, ill-fitting, wrong.

All I wanted was to be back home, lying on my couch in my pajamas.

As I walked down the aisle, I discerned a different type of air. It was fresher, cooler, more invigorating. I gained energy as I breathed and began to think maybe I would be all right after all.

"Go, Mom. Go. You have to keep walking." I must have stopped, unaware, as if frozen in time.

She squeezed right past me, leaving me behind as she plowed ahead, glancing back with her ice-castle eyes that pulled me forward. I followed, stopping every few feet to mop up the tears. Would I know these strangers? Would they know me? Would they see what a mess I was? And if they did, would they be able to like me? I so desperately wanted them to like me. *To Love Me.* The questions and fears raged inside me as I focused on moving forward, just one step in front of the other. I propelled myself through the dull, gray walkway and felt as if I was traveling down the birth canal once again, working toward the painful expulsion into life and the unknown.

I stopped when I reached the entrance to the terminal; it seemed a fitting word to describe the space I was about to enter. The years of gestation were over, but what was about to take its place would be as irrevocable as death itself.

I stared out over the different-colored heads that were milling about, greeting family with excitement, until my eyes landed on two heads that were unmoving, fixed on the gaping entrance to the walkway.

Our brown eyes connected like magnets as they locked in place. In a flash of understanding, I instantly knew why I had never fit in anywhere before. In those eyes, I saw something I had never seen before, as genetic markers exploded from my cells toward their matches. I saw, for the first time, my own eyes, looking back at me.

Who in the world am I? Ah, that's the great puzzle.
—Lewis Carroll, *Alice in Wonderland*

Chapter 13

The Looking Glass

"Hi, I'm Carol," my sister said as she gave me a warm hug. "And this is our brother, Jim."

Jim gave me an awkward hug and we all stood there for a moment, staring.

"I ... I ... can't believe it," I finally said and then burst into tears, another string of salty pearls that tumbled silently onto the concrete floors. Carol and Jim wrapped their arms around me in a family embrace, unlike anything I'd ever experienced before, and then Jim released us and stepped away, as Carol and I continued to look at each other with wonder.

Just beyond us, as a new niece, my daughter was already chatting away with her Uncle Jim. I wanted to lap up every word and not let a single syllable get away, but it was impossible to follow both conversations at once. That's when I realized we were practically the only ones left in the terminal, our little family reunion like an island of people in a lonely airport gate, all the other travelers having moved on.

"Let's sit outside for a few minutes before you leave to go to your hotel," Carol said, her arm still around me.

"Oh, good idea," I said. I felt like I was in a dream where I didn't quite know which part to play, so I simply followed her instructions, and we all walked through the airport to an exit that took us outside. I inhaled the cool, moist air and felt immediately relieved. A row of palm trees lined the walk before us, rising from colorful beds of reds and yellows peppered with bursts of brilliant blues. Even in the evening twilight, the beauty of the city was evident. Carol pulled me toward a bench at the side of the cement wall. My new brother and his new niece had already disappeared.

I tried to focus on the woman in front of me—my sister. The word bounced around in my brain, trying to find a place to land. My brain had never had to make room for such a concept before, but now, miraculously, here she was.

This is my sister … This is my sister … This is my sister Carol.

I kept saying the words to myself as our mouths mumbled small talk. I couldn't take my eyes off of her. I studied her face as I'd never studied anyone before, except for my daughter's when she was first born. The woman who was my sister and standing before me in British Columbia had the same face shape as mine. Inside her face was a smile that crinkled in the same place as mine. We had the same eyebrows, the same cowlick, and the same teeth. Her hair was cut short, just a bit longer than mine. It was the same color that mine had once been, before it had begun turning gray. Her makeup had been applied faultlessly; mascara was on her long lashes and her lips were the perfect color. But it was otherwise practically the same face as my own, bare one. I couldn't stop staring at her: I half expected her to dissolve before my very eyes, like a dream.

Carol pulled me down beside her and we continued to stare at each other awkwardly, not knowing where to begin, until before long, the tears were flowing down both our faces. We both had so many questions, a whole century of life between us to catch up on.

My daughter and Jim appeared from somewhere in the darkening night. As I watched them walk toward us, I stared at my brother and felt his confusion and wonder, as well. He was tall like me and wore glasses. With his mustache and muscle shirt, he reminded me of one of the gentle bikers that took care of me when I was sick so very long ago. I noticed a labyrinth of laugh lines surrounding his eyes and was grateful to know that laughter lived in his house. As I looked at him, I saw myself again, and again, I was shocked to see my reflection in a stranger's face. As we all stood there, not knowing what to do or say next, I realized that with the three-hour time difference, it was way past midnight for us. Our bodies would need a couple of days to adjust to this new time zone. And my mind would need a couple of decades to adjust to this new life zone.

"I guess we should go to the hotel now," I said. We'd arranged a rental car and I still had to go to the kiosk and get the keys, which I knew would either go smoothly or take half the night, so it was best to take care of it and get settled in. Besides, I didn't think I could take another moment of the emotional explosion I felt inside me.

"Oh, sure, of course," Carol said. "We have a lifetime to catch up. Laura's probably going to be dropping by your hotel to meet you after she gets off work tonight," she added. "So I hope you're ready for more family!"

"I don't know how ready I'll ever be," I said, "but I can't wait to meet her!" But inside, as true as it was that I couldn't wait to meet her, I was afraid if I saw one more sibling I just might implode with excitement and terror.

We embraced one more time, and I watched as they walked to their car. There was something so familiar in how they walked. Just as in how they talked, and how they smiled. How could that be, when we didn't even know each other, I wondered. I noticed the lush abundance of the trees and flowers that framed them as their silhouettes disappeared from my view and marveled at how much more alive British Columbia felt, compared to the cold, bleak, wintery landscape of Ontario. Everything suddenly felt so very much alive. And for the first time in my life, so did I.

Lost in my thoughts, I suddenly felt a finger poking my leg. "Come on, Mom. It's really late. We have to get going." With the ease of the young, she flung both of our packs over her shoulders and pulled me to a stand. We wandered first to the rental kiosk, and then to the parking lot where our rental car would be found. As we searched for the car, my body cried out in exhaustion. We had been traveling for more than twelve hours, first in the train, then the cab to the airport, then the plane and now, in a rental car in an unfamiliar city. I wished I could just close my eyes and wake up in a soft, warm bed.

"There it is," she declared and pointed to a nondescript blue hatchback. We threw our packs in the backseat and climbed inside. And that's when I broke down.

Sitting behind the wheel of the unmoving car, I sobbed and sobbed, a whole lifetime of emptiness howling to be undone. These were the brother and sisters I'd never had, the brother and sisters whose birthdays and Christmases I'd never shared, the brother and sisters I'd never had the chance to squabble with, much less to love. Left alone in that big house in Belleville with a woman who never knew how to love or be a mother, I suddenly felt that gaping wound of my birth open wide, wider than it had ever been opened before. For the first time in my life, my loss was no longer in my imagination but had stood before me in the flesh. I'd seen and held the brother and sister I was never allowed.

"Are you okay, Mom?"

"I'll be fine," I said between sobs. "I'm just overwhelmed, is all."

"I know," she said, laying her hand gently on my knee. "It's going to be okay."

I shook off the last of the sobs, unfolded the map, and focused on where we had to drive. Then, in the dark of the night, we began our journey into a new world.

After we'd reached the hotel and checked in, I handed her the key. "Here, you go on up. I just need a minute."

She nodded, grabbed the packs, and headed for the elevator. I watched her hair bounce off her shoulders with the energy of the young and longed to have a bit of that youthful exuberance for myself. When the elevators closed, I walked outside and saw an ashtray stand, just what I was looking for. I leaned against a pillar and reached into my purse for a pack of cigarettes, telling myself once again that I really had to quit. Since finding out about my birth mother's diagnosis with emphysema, the reality was obvious. Just as I struck the match, a car pulled into the parking lot, the heads inside swiveling in my direction as it passed by me. A loud screech of tires and a rapid drive backward about fifty feet brought me face to face with another woman who looked like me.

"I knew it was you!" she screamed from the driver's window. She jumped out of the car and her long, blonde hair flew behind her like golden wings. Before I could say anything, she pulled me into a long embrace, and for the second time that evening, my genetic markers leapt into action, finding their counterparts in this alien woman who seemed as excited as I was terrified. It was my sister Laura. She had just gotten off her shift as a psychiatric nurse—we had both chosen the same career, a twist of fate that brought us immediately together.

Within seconds, we were joking about our jobs, and then before we knew it, we were comparing noses. After a few minutes of this, one of her kids shut off the car and they both climbed out, and more introductions were made.

"Auntie Claire," a good-looking boy about my daughter's age said. "I'm David, and this is Lisa."

I stared into their eyes, caught off guard by being called "Auntie." I had never been anyone's aunt before, had never even conceived of such a role. But now, suddenly, as I stood in the parking lot having a smoke, it slowly dawned on me that having a new family also meant having a whole new identity to get used to.

"I'm an aunt!" I blurted out, not even intending to speak my thoughts out loud. My face flushed as a broad smile stretched across my face. "I've never been an aunt!"

I couldn't believe the words I was hearing. Some more chatter followed, and then I realized my daughter was waiting for me in our room.

"Come on," I told them. "Let's go up; your cousin is waiting!" After they parked the car, we all crowded into the elevator, where our eyes moved from face to face and back again, each of us examining the other for recognizable markers.

My daughter was delighted to meet her cousins and aunt, and I watched with indescribable pride as a new generation of bonding commenced. Questions were rapidly fired back and forth, but the answers tumbled from our mouths more slowly as we tried to condense our lifetimes into a few moments of late-night babble.

"We'll figure it out later," Laura said as she realized how exhausted we were. I'd been so excited the night before we left that I hadn't gotten any sleep at all, and the realization that it had been twenty-four hours since I'd slept made me all the more giddy with exhaustion. I had to crash, and my daughter did, too. I could tell as I watched her head start to nod on her shoulders like a bobble-head doll.

After they left, we got ready for bed, and I put all the amazing discoveries of the night into my Wall of Secrets, where I could pull them out and examine them more carefully another time. I tossed and turned in the unfamiliar bed and then finally focused on my breath and let sleep make its way into my electrified mind.

Hours later, my hands explored my face and pushed my eyes wide open. *Where am I?* I wondered for a moment. Slowly, the memories of the previous amazing night came back to me. I stretched my legs and realized that every muscle in my body ached as I wiggled my toes and flexed my calves. I'd sat for so long on the train and the plane that my body had practically frozen into a fetal position. How appropriate, I thought, as I realized that this was the day I would meet *my mother. My real mother,* the one who carried me in her womb for nine long months, who pushed me through her body into the world, the one who gave me life.

As my eyes adjusted to the room, I gazed around and saw the sunshine flowing through the cracks of the blinds. It didn't seem possible that it was already daybreak, but the hands on the clock confirmed it. They also confirmed how little sleep I'd had, as I'd tossed and turned through the half-night that was left for sleeping once my sister and nephew and niece had left.

My sister and nephew and niece. The words still bewildered me. I shook my head as if I could shake off the shock, but still, it was there. I looked over to the other bed and saw my daughter. She was sleeping quietly, deeply, and peacefully. How could she be so peaceful, when I felt so terrified, I wondered? Were we not connected through birth ourselves? How could she not feel the anxiety coursing through me?

Then I laughed at my own thoughts. It was almost as if I wanted her to share my anxiety. How could I wish this fear and worry on anyone, least of all my daughter? Surely, I didn't want her to carry the weight of my world within her, and yet, my anxiety felt so incomprehensibly loud that I couldn't imagine how she could sleep through it.

I swung my reluctant legs out of the bed, reached over, and peeked through the blinds. Brilliant sunlight flooded the gardens that were full of unusual plants and flowers unlike any I'd seen before. Their vibrant colors and shapes were a bright accent to this momentous day, reinforcing the newness of all that was about to happen.

I stood up and stretched my arms to the heavens, my hands practically touching the ceiling. Everything hurt—my legs, my back, and my heart. I couldn't quite understand why I felt in so much emotional pain. I thought, if anything, I should be filled with joy. But just as in the car when I broke down and sobbed after meeting Carol and Jim, this morning brought with it more of that infinite anguish that came of knowing how much love and affection had been denied me. And knowing I was about to meet the woman who had made that decision to deny me filled me with a deep and terrible ache that I so desperately wanted to heal.

I quietly tiptoed around the room and got the coffee started. Then I opened the balcony door and slipped outside for my morning smoke. Just as I was about to close the sliding glass doors, my daughter rolled over and punched her pillow with annoyance.

"What are you doing, Mom?" she asked rhetorically. "You can't smoke here. Put it out. Go back to sleep." Her words hit me like little darts, and I closed the sliding glass door and moved closer to the balcony's edge, away from the word *darts*, away from the pain.

I lit my cigarette and inhaled its smoke, and I looked down on the people in the parking lot below as they filled their trunks with luggage and headed back home. As I took in the smell of the ocean air, I marveled at how far we'd come, both in geography and life. I never thought this day would happen, and I wanted to memorize every single second.

I stepped back into the room and saw that she had gone back to sleep. The gurgling coffee pot told me the coffee was ready. I poured a hot, steaming cup and looked over at her, noting the spikes of reddish, twisted hair jutting out from her head that made her look like a creature from the unknown. I thought of how dearly I loved her and wished for her to have the family I never had. Hot pearls pooled in the corners of my eyes, and I quickly tried to push them back inside. I missed a few, and they bounced onto my cheeks and then dribbled down onto my pajama top. *Enough already!* I thought to myself. *I must stay focused. Today is the day. Today is the day I will finally meet her.*

I looked down and realized I hadn't even taken a sip of my coffee. My fingers had wrapped themselves around the steaming cup, and I embraced its warmth. The first sip was bitter, but it awoke my taste buds from their jet lag. As the caffeine slid down my throat, I considered the new words I'd now made my own. *Sister. Brother. Aunt. Nephew. Niece.* Words that had been empty of meaning throughout my life were now terribly intimate and joyous. The words of my new reality wound themselves around and around inside my brain, tangling into a ball of disorder and confusion, like a foreign language that required my full attention. But like a foreign language, the knowledge that I could master it and turn the incomprehensible syllables into something with meaning and import was exciting.

I finished my coffee and contemplated my new vocabulary. I was in a new place, learning a new language, with new people. This was their world.

And one among them would be a most familiar word but would now take on an entirely unfamiliar meaning. *Mother.* I would learn a new meaning for a word that had for so long filled me with such dread.

"Mother."

It was my daughter. She was waking up. "Hello? Mom?" I shook off my thoughts and looked at her as she sat upright, her tousled, twisted, spiky hair like a wreath around her face.

"Oh, sorry, I was just thinking."

"Well, stop thinking," she said. "You're so lost in your daydreams, you didn't even hear me. Besides, you don't have time for thinking. This is the day you get to meet your birth mom!"

I smiled. She hadn't been oblivious. Maybe she understood me better than I realized. I don't know why it surprised me. After all, we were connected by birth.

And my thoughts drifted back to my own mother and all that the day would bring.

As she showered, I wondered what the meeting with my mother would be like. How would I react? How would she react? What would I say? What would she say? What would she look like? What would her voice sound like? Would she hug me? Would she hold me and tell me she loved me and that she was sorry she gave me away?

As my thoughts meandered, I became aware of the traffic outside as it grew louder, noisier. The city sounds had replaced the calming night sounds. The day was about to begin, whether I was ready for it or not. A seagull lit on the balcony's edge and stared at me. I stared back. It was so much larger than the gulls on the East Coast. This one was huge, the size of an eagle, I thought. It cocked its head as it stared at me, as if to ask, "What's wrong?"

"What do you think I should wear to meet my mother?" I asked him with a smile. In answer, he ruffled his feathers, settled comfortably on the railing, and watched me with his black, beady eyes. He wanted me to make my own decision.

Comfort. That's what I needed, I realized. I needed to be as comfortable as possible, so rather than dressing to impress, I would dress to maximize my comfort during this most uncomfortable day.

"It will have to be my old favorites," I told my seagull. Jeans and a white shirt. He seemed to nod in agreement, and I pulled a pair of jeans and a clean, white shirt from my suitcase and got dressed. I laughed as I realized I'd asked a bird for fashion advice. *What will my new family think of me talking to animals and birds?* I wondered. They'd probably think their new sister was a bit unusual, I concluded.

Sister. There's that new word again. *Sister.* Just saying it to myself sent chills up my arm. I turned to the window, and as I did so, my seagull friend flew off and landed on the adjacent balcony, where he pecked for some crumbs of food. I felt comforted knowing he was still near, as if he were a guardian sent to comfort and calm me on this magical, momentous day.

What should I call her? Could I call her Mom? Mother? Marilyn? Should I ask her why she gave me away but kept the others? Should I ask her why she didn't look for me all those years? So many years of questions.

I opened the blinds to let in the sun's rays that seemed so eager to please and lit up another cigarette. I leaned out the balcony door and blew smoke into the air, wishing my fears would float away with each puff.

"Mom!" I heard a scream from behind the bathroom door. "Stop smoking in here! You'll get us kicked out!"

"Leave me alone," I snapped back. "You don't get it." I didn't know where my anger was coming from, or why I so readily hurled it at my daughter. But my anger was deep, and when I caught a glimpse of myself in the mirror, I saw that my face was fixed in a snarl.

I heard her slamming around in the bathroom, her own anger apparent, and I knew the day had officially begun. I hungrily sucked back several cigarettes before she emerged all scrubbed and shiny, drying her hair in a hotel towel. She seems to have forgotten both our angers.

"Your turn now," she says cheerfully. "Are you excited to meet your mother?"

"Honey," I say quietly, calmed by the cigarettes and my thoughts. "I'm terrified beyond words. I have this huge body of pain that is so intense there are no words to describe it." I was speaking calmly, methodically, as if discussing the contents of my suitcase and not the contents of my soul. Somehow, the detached tone of my voice helped me to keep a safe distance from my pain, but I knew it was a distance that could be bridged in an instant with the power of my emotions. Wherever that bottomless pit of grief was coming from, I knew I had to keep it at bay, had to reign in the growing pain in my soul and my flooding emotions long enough to just make it through the day.

"You should be happy," she said, her innocence and confusion apparent in her tone. She really didn't understand why I was feeling so much pain on what should be such a happy occasion. And in some ways, neither did I. For years, I'd lived with it, but I thought it would be snuffed out when I found my birth family, not enflamed.

I turned away and lit another cigarette so that I could hide my tears and frustration in a fog of swirling smoke. When I closed my eyes, the Wall of Secrets appeared, as vivid as if I could reach right out and touch it. There was one drawer left, a huge one. It was open and beckoned me to jump inside, to put my whole being inside it and slam the drawer shut forever.

I remembered all the drawers of terrors and secrets that I'd tucked away, hauling them out again and again, experiencing the fear and shame and unrelenting pain over and over as if for the first time. If I could relive each moment that went into a drawer, I reasoned, perhaps I could find a way out of the pain. Respond a different way. Feel it a different way. Understand it in a different way. But each time, it felt the same. Each time, I relived the hurt and shoved the pain back into its drawer, slammed it shut, and closed my eyes.

My spiritual teachers had told me I had to find internal peace. Peace that would match what I portrayed on the outside. It seemed an impossible task, with so many drawers begging to be opened.

Blinking rapidly, I tried to resist the temptation to shove myself into the drawers. I opened my eyes and let in the golden rays of sunshine, like rays of hope.

"I'll be ready in a few minutes," I said to her, knowing she was still confused and upset with me as she dressed and put on her makeup, ready to meet her new grandmother. She now had a whole new family today, aunts, uncles, and cousins. I watched her and I knew I was throwing a blanket of darkness over what should be a vibrant, exciting day, and I only wished that she could understand why I held that blanket.

Later, as I stood in the shower, I released the fears and tensions that had already accumulated since I woke. As the hot water flowed, it washed away the grime of despair and sent it swiftly down the drain. I so desperately wanted to restart the day fresh and new, to step out of the shower a new and happy woman. I scrubbed my skin until every cell was new; I let the water flow clear and clean for what seemed like hours.

"Come on, Mom!" she said as she banged on the door. "Hurry up! I'm starving!"

"All right, I'm coming! Hold your horses," I shout back.

I turned off the water, climbed out of the shower, and dried myself off. With the corner of my towel, I made circles on the steam-covered mirror. The face that emerged looked the same as the face I had seen the day before. Tired and drawn tight with stress. The day I would meet my mother was a day filled with fear. It would have to do.

When I was dressed and ready to go, I patted my pockets, then shook and looked into my purse. It was as if I was looking for something, like I'd forgotten something, but I didn't know what. Clothed on the outside, I appeared ready for the day. But on the inside, I was naked and unprepared.

"Let's go, Mom," she ordered, her patience long gone. "We need to eat and get to your mom's house."

My mom's house. Only this time, the phrase didn't bring me waves of anxiety, didn't fill me with dread. It was not the house in Belleville I'd grown up in. It was a house in British Columbia, and the original house that I wasn't allowed to grow up in was in Alberta. It wasn't my house.

I looked up at her as she waited for me, her purse hanging from her shoulders and the door key in her hand. She was ready. I let my eyes take in her beauty. My daughter was strong and charismatic. Like a Viking warrior, she waited for me, her eyes shining with excitement.

I had to put away my thoughts about my own mother and accept my role as her mother. It was time to feed my child.

But inside, I didn't feel like a mother. I felt like a newborn child.

Wholeness is not achieved by cutting off a portion of one's being …
But by integration of the contraries.

—Carl Jung

Chapter 14

The Birthing

I have no memory of breakfast; the meal passed by in a blur of activity inside my brain. "I'm not ready for this," I said as we walked toward the car.

"You'll be fine," She said as she took hold of my arm and pulled me along. I struggled to resist, but she had taken charge. "Geez, Mom, you really have to get it together."

I halted and glared at her, our eyes fixed on each other. "This is really hard. I know you don't understand what it all means to me, but you need to have patience and compassion." She rolled her eyes and walked ahead. I felt crushed by her rejection and impatience.

"You okay to drive?" she asked when we reached the car.

"Of course I am!" I flung the words at her like snapping a wet towel in her direction. We climbed in the car silently, both of us fuming. Every muscle in my body was clenched and tense. I pulled out the map—the map that would take me to my mother—and we studied it together. In map language, it was an inch away. *I'm so close to seeing my mother, yet so far away from knowing her.* The thoughts overtook my mind, scampering around like annoying rodents I couldn't shut out.

I hesitated as I wrapped my fingers around the key in the ignition. They froze in position and would not move.

"Turn it," she instructed. "Come on, Mom, turn the key."

"Okay, okay, give me a minute," I said. She let out a big sigh of frustration, and I obediently turned the key. As the motor purred in eagerness for its journey, I breathed deeply, in and out, in and out. *Breathe ... breathe ... breathe,* I told myself as I fixed my eyes on the road, cast my ears toward her spoken directions, and clamped my hands tightly on the wheel.

"Turn left here," she told me, and I did as she instructed.

"And you're going to make a right at that next light," she said, and I slowed down. "We're almost there! It's right around the corner!" Her excitement was building, as was my fear. I wanted to pull over to the side of the road and just stop, but I knew if I did that, she would be annoyed. I didn't want to dampen her excitement any further.

But I could barely stand the thought that we were almost there. *Any minute now,* I told myself, *and we will be there. I will be standing before my mother.*

I slowed to a crawl and pretended to admire the lovely homes, the flowers in the gardens, the decorated porches. "Look," I said, pointing to the right. "Palm trees! And what are those beautiful bushes of pink?"

"Quit stalling, Mom," she ordered.

I was frozen in time. And then I saw it. The number to Carol's house, where my mother would be waiting. We'd reached it.

"Okay, we're here now," I said as I pulled in the driveway and breathed deeply. My child bounded out of the car before I'd even unfastened my seatbelt. I moved in slow motion as I uncurled my legs and climbed out. I straightened up, like a fern uncurling in the forest, and I stood tall and willed my legs to move. My eyes scanned the picture before me. A neatly manicured lawn held a little bungalow covered in silver-gray stucco. The sun's rays struck the corner and the stucco sparkled like diamonds, giving it a magical cast that couldn't have been more perfect for the moment. The lawn was a carpet of brilliant greens as lush as a velvet painting. The shrubs were manicured into precise box forms, and the bushes, recently clipped to encourage new growth, sat like guards on either side of the porch. A black wrought-iron railing led up to the door.

The door to my mother.

My daughter leapt up the few stairs leading to the door, and before I could yell, "Wait!" she had lifted her fist to knock. Then, before her knuckles could reach the door, it opened, just a crack.

A sharp inhalation of air pulled my organs tightly together, squeezing the life from me. "Oh, my God!" I said out loud, in a whoosh as I expelled my breath and my organs slipped back into place. With herculean determination, I forced my foot to take a step forward, and then another, and another. With each step forward, the door opened another inch. Everything was in slow motion, but still, it wasn't slow enough. In the few seconds that felt like hours, I arrived at the stairs. By the time I climbed them the door had opened wide. And I stood, face to face, with the woman who had given me life.

Her face was weathered and crinkled with age, but gentle. Her illness had left her skin very pale, almost ashen, and the tube running from her nose to her oxygen tank was a stark reminder of just how ill she truly was. Silver curls framed a face that was the most beautiful sight I had ever seen. *My mother.* Her watery brown eyes swirled with mystery and sadness as she gazed at me, her unknown daughter.

I felt seized by panic and disbelief, but still, excited and overjoyed. A flood of emotion engulfed me, while snippets of conversation flew in and out of my ears as cousins and aunts greeted their new relative. But all I could focus on was the woman who stood before me. She was the same height as me, but she was slighter in build, like a willowy tree waving in the wind. I feared she could topple over at any moment. I saw that in her fist, she held fast to her lifeline to her oxygen tubing.

"Hello," she said, hesitantly. "I'm … Marilyn. Your mother." A thunderous silence fell like a wall between us, and then, in an instant, it lifted. "Come in, come in," she said warmly as she stepped away from the doorway. Her voice was like coffee with a splash of bourbon. It warmed my heart immediately.

I entered, turned toward her, and without thinking, reached out and wrapped my arms around her shoulders. Holding her frail, skeletal frame in my hands, I whispered in her ear, "It's so good to meet you."

A shaky hand reached to my waist in response and she whispered back, "You too." Then she stepped away.

A flurry of people surrounded me and hugs were passed again with my new siblings and niece and nephews. Carol guided us to the kitchen and suggested we sit down at the kitchen table. It was a small, round, white table set beneath a window. Just outside the window, I noticed a carefully trimmed garden. It reminded me of the watch post my adopted mother had spent her remaining years gazing out to. But this one had a softer, safer feel, almost as if the garden were watching over the people inside, instead of the people inside, watching out.

My new mother arranged her lifeline in coils around her and sat down. I pulled out a chair and sat beside her.

"Coffee?" Carol asked, breaking the awkward silence. "Would you like some coffee?"

"Sure, thanks," I answered. I was mesmerized by my mother and sucked in every image of her face through my eyes.

"Auntie Claire," I heard Carol say, "these are my sons." Reluctantly, I moved my eyes from my mother to meet my new nephews, Paul and Jamie, two handsome young men almost my daughter's age. We shared awkward greetings, and then, I turned once again to my mother.

So many things were happening all at once. I couldn't focus or follow the many conversations that were flowing from room to room. Many pairs of eyes were watching me, including my new mother's.

"Look!" Carol said. "You're both wearing the same thing!" She gestured toward us both, and my mother and I looked at each other and laughed.

"This is my official uniform," I said. "I always end up wearing jeans and a white shirt when I don't know what else to put on."

"I do, too!" my new mother said with a smile.

"Isn't that interesting?" Carol said. "I wonder what else we all have in common?"

"I'm sure there are many things that are the same," my mother said. As I looked into her eyes and let my own eyes wander across the unfamiliar territory of her face, I saw myself etched in her flesh.

The unfamiliar face was so familiar. Like looking in a mirror, I was reflected back. *This is my mother,* I said to myself as I studied her. But the words felt so abstract, as if a part of me still didn't know what the words meant.

"Would you like to see some albums?" Carol asked. I looked up at her, confused. "Photo albums," she explained.

"Oh, sure, yes, yes, of course," I answered. And then a rush of sadness swept over me, as I realized that I would need to see photograph albums to know my family history. Albums that captured, for eternity, the love and joys and lives of the family that I had been excluded from, since the day that I was born.

My daughter appeared in the doorway, her new cousins in tow. "How are you doing, Mom?" she asked.

"Okay. I'm okay," I answered with a weak smile, knowing the words were far from the truth. I looked out to the backyard so I could avoid eye contact with her. I knew that if our eyes connected, she would see my confusion and sadness. The brief glimpse of nature helped to settle me. I marveled at the many different greens of the Pacific Coast, so unlike the two or three shades of green in Ontario. There were so many plants and trees I didn't recognize. Even the windowsill held flowers I wasn't familiar with. Everything was so foreign: the surroundings, the family, and most of all, the confusing emotions. I had thought that meeting my mother would still my emotions, fill me with pure joy, but there was so much sadness, pain, and confusion alongside the joy that I couldn't focus on any of them.

I wanted to learn about these strangers that I now called family. If I studied them, came to know them, the emotions might settle. I would find peace. Every small detail became important, helped me to understand who I was and where I had come from. As I glanced around, I noticed that Carol and I had similar tastes. Similar colors lived in my house. Earthy tones filled the space in Carol's home very well. Even some of her furniture was like mine. I found the similarities intriguing. Were they coincidence, because we were nearly the same age, or were they something deeper, more mysterious? I so wanted to know.

As I moved my eyes back toward my mother, I found her staring at me. I sucked in a breath and looked back. As I searched her brown eyes, I saw the same confusion and fear that I knew she saw in mine. We also had the same deep, dark sadness so obvious to others.

"Thank you for letting me come to meet you," I whispered. "I know this must be just as difficult for you as it is for me."

Her eyes were shiny with unshed tears. "It's okay," she said, pulling back into herself. "Oh, look, Carol has the photo albums. Let's look."

The moment had passed in avoidance. The child within me desperately wished a mother's arms would wrap around my shoulders with a warm embrace of welcome. But I realized that it wasn't going to happen. After all the years of longing, and finally finding her, that maternal protection wouldn't be offered—only pleasantries, nothing more.

In an instant, I realized that the mothering that I so desperately needed didn't live there. It wasn't going to come from the woman who had turned me out, carried and bore me and then returned home alone, unencumbered by a child. She didn't have the love inside of her to give to me, and no amount of longing could possibly change that. She lived in my heart, and I lived nowhere.

Carol piled several photo albums in the middle of the table. With shaky hands, my mother took the first one on the pile. As she turned the pages looking for the pictures she wanted to share with me, I watched Carol, watching me. Everyone was struggling to find the right words, the right place, and the right fit.

"I'm glad you're here," Carol said with a reassuring hand on my shoulder.

"Thank you. I am, too," I said, as warm tears filled my eyes. Laughter erupted in the background; it came from the living room and filled the silent gaps in our conversation. I was so happy that my daughter had found her place among this new family so quickly. But I still struggled to find mine.

"Look, this is me when I was just a young girl," my mother said, pointing to a picture of someone who looked like a 1940s movie star.

"That is so beautiful," I said in awe. She then told a story of the years she spent working during the war, and a new light shone in her eyes. As she spoke of her youth, her face became illuminated by her happy memories.

"And that is your father," she said, watching for my reaction.

The picture she pointed to was small, and it was difficult to make out his face. I was eager to see him, to search for similarities in our faces.

"Do you have any others?" I asked her. "Bigger ones?"

"No, this is it," she said as she turned the page. I glanced over to Carol, hoping for some answers reflected in her eyes. She pursed her lips and gave a small shake of her head, making it clear that the subject was best dropped for the time being.

We moved on to other photos, and I was shown my mother's trips to Mexico with her friends, adventures she took on cruises, trail rides in the Rockies. When she came to a series of photos of her saddling up for rides, the images jumped from the page, straight to my heart.

"I just love horses!" I told her as I looked lovingly at the pictures.

"You do?" my mother asked.

"Oh, my goodness, yes. I would have loved to have been around them and been able to ride with you," I said with a sigh.

"I love them, too," she said with a smile as she remembered her horse-riding days. "Your sisters didn't care much for them, though."

My thoughts flashed to the painful realization that I could have been her riding companion when I was growing up. I again felt the warm tears in my eyes and bit my lip to hold them back.

Another album was opened. It held pictures of their family at different times in their lives: Christmases and birthdays being celebrated, graduations and family reunions.

"We'll make our own new memories," Carol said, sensing my distress.

"I know," I said. "It's just so overwhelming."

"And this page is in Viking, where we lived for awhile." My mother pointed to a picture of a house.

"Viking?" I asked, incredulously. "What years were you there?"

Carol did some fast calculating in her head and told me. I had visited my adopted family there one summer when I was little, one of the same summers they'd been living there. After several questions back and forth, we realized that they had gone to school with my adoptive cousin. We had even probably all played on the same playground when I was visiting. We were so close, but we never even knew it—never even knew of each other's existence.

Another page of family history held in another album was shown and talked about, and I stared in amazement at the similarities between my mother's youthful face and my own. Even pictures of my sisters when they were younger looked remarkably like me.

After some time, I began to shift in my chair as I felt a powerful fatigue come over me. My mother closed the last book of memories, and I saw that she, too, was exhausted. My eyes wandered up her face, hoping to engage her eyes in some kind of a connection, but the instant our eyes touched, she looked away.

She is as broken as I am, I thought. *Her soul has been shattered by the loss of a child.*

She struggled to get up rapidly and sucked in the needed oxygen from the skinny tubing. I jumped up to help her, finding comfort in my nurse's role.

"Here, let me give you a hand," I said.

"I can manage, thank you," she said as she wound up the tubing so she could walk around. I watched her maneuver her oxygen tubing down the hall, pretending to be strong.

"She's just like me," I said to Carol. "Won't let anyone help. Fiercely independent."

"Yes, to the point that it makes looking after her pretty difficult," Carol replied. We shared a smile, and I was grateful for her understanding.

I had so many questions demanding so many answers. They couldn't be asked all at once, but I still felt a sense of urgency after waiting so many years. I watched again as my mother returned down the hall, holding her roll of tubing. Seeing how frail and ill my mother was, I knew she wouldn't live much longer. *I finally found you,* I thought, *and now you are leaving this world.* It was incomprehensible to know that.

She sat back down and arranged the tubing neatly in an adjacent chair.

"I hope sometime we can go through these albums again," I told her.

She smiled and replied, "Of course. Whenever you want. Do you think you will come back soon?"

Inside, I was howling to be heard, wanting to scream out, *you want me back?* I so desperately wanted her to open her arms and call me back, to call me back from half a century of longing, to snatch me back from the arms of the hospital attendants who took me away.

But all I said was, "Maybe in the fall, when I take more holidays."

I knew I would stay forever if I was wanted and if I mattered in their lives. But before I could let the thought linger any longer, my sister Laura burst in the room, on her way to work. Our conversation instantly took on a lighter note as work-related questions replaced the memories of the past. It felt comforting to have something concrete to discuss, something other than the family I'd been excluded from.

We moved to the living room, and I watched my mother's eyes roam from one person to the next. It was the first time she had seen her children together in one place. It was the first time I had seen my birth family, all in one place. *This is what it should look like,* I thought. *The energy is touchable and static with connections.*

Eyes connected with eyes, transferring the needed information and filling the holes that had been empty for so long. My brother, Jim, interrupted the heavy atmosphere with a joke, and the mood shifted to laughter, with conversation springing up and flying back and forth as if we'd always known each other.

How can people who have never met be so similar and intrinsically connected in voice and manner? I wondered. There was an internal knowing of each other that was shocking. I stared and watched in disbelief as their mannerisms, senses of humor, ways of walking, all reflected my and my daughter's own.

Eventually, Laura had to leave, and we decided to take pictures on the front lawn. It was my first family picture ever, and again, I choked back tears. We took turns in twos and threes and fours, with everyone smiling and posing for the camera. When it was finally over, I knew I had to have copies of the photos as soon as possible, to take home the waxy paper images of my family to assure myself that it was real.

As we went back in the house, the exhaustion on my face was apparent. "I think we should go soon," I announced to everyone and no one.

"Okay, okay. Let's make plans for tomorrow, then," Carol said. I searched my mother's eyes for something, anything that would send me the message to stay.

"I'm tired, too," she said, as she struggled for air from just a walk to the door.

"Can I see you just for a minute?" I asked her. I was shocked that the words had fallen out of my mouth; I hadn't planned to say them.

What was I thinking? What was I going to say?

The thought of being alone with my birth mother somehow terrified me, and I felt a choking sensation and heaviness of emotion surging upward, as if ready to burst from me at any second.

I forced my emotions to stay calm. My hand grasped hers, and I stared in disbelief at our entwined fingers. As my sobs erupted through our silence, I pulled her into a small room off the kitchen.

"Here," I said through my sobs, "sit down here for a minute." I knelt before her, wanting reassurance that I was free to speak. She sat upright, stiffly, holding her plastic tubing. Her eyes avoided mine and instead watched the shadows on the wall. Inside, I was screaming to be heard, once again.

Please, please, just love me! Just tell me this is all okay. Tell me you want me here. Tell me I belong in this family and you've missed me.

What actually fell out of my mouth for her to hear were only a few sentences. "I need you to know that I'm not angry," I said, swallowing scalding-hot tears. "But why didn't you ever look for me?"

"I thought you would be terribly angry," she said, shyly looking around my face, still avoiding my eyes. "I didn't think you would want to meet me, and I didn't want to interfere in your life." She spoke in a whisper, her words barely audible.

"My life?" I said. "My life has been lived in hell. I've been searching for you forever."

"I didn't know," she said, looking at the door, clearly wanting to escape.

"I have so much to ask you, so much to talk to you about," I told her.

She nodded and silence filled the room that grew smaller, crowding out my wants and needs, replacing them with walls.

As my mother struggled to stand, I understood that the moment was over. I turned into a nurse and collected the tubing and put my arm under hers to help her ambulate, as if she were my patient. Our physical connection vibrated with uncertainty, a flickering tension that reminded me that she was not my patient, nor I, her nurse. We were mother and daughter, role-playing.

I turned briefly, and our eyes met. I smiled shyly and she smiled in return, as she stepped forward, back into the comfort of her family. If only she knew I blamed her for nothing and forgave her for everything.

There is sacredness in tears. They are not the
mark of weakness but of power.
They speak more eloquently than ten thousand tongues.
They are messengers of overwhelming grief,
And unspeakable love.
—Washington Irving

Chapter 15

The Crossing

"I met her. I met my mother. Oh, my God!" I pulled the words out of my mouth; they had been stuck in my mouth for so long, cemented by my tears. I didn't know where the pain was coming from—I had been back home for days, the visit like a fleeting dream, my memories disintegrating with each passing day until I pulled out my pen and began recalling every detail. But as the memories were recorded, they brought more pain. I wrapped my arms around my knees as I lay in a fetal position, rocking back and forth, trying to comfort myself. A secret place had opened up—a dark and primal wound so open and raw, I couldn't imagine it ever healing.

Alone with my thoughts, I questioned the relevance of my suffering. Life is not without suffering of some kind. It doesn't mean that something is necessarily wrong. It just usually means we are clinging to the hope that things will be different. I had so wanted things to be different, for my mother to reach out and hold me tight to her chest and bury her face in my hair and tell me she loved me, that I was her child, that she was sorry she had abandoned me, that she never wanted me to go to such an unloving home.

But she did none of that. She was polite—kind, even—but her discomfort was palpable. She didn't view me as her child, but as a visitor, more like a distant relative who had shown up at her door one day than as her long-lost daughter. I was at best, a curiosity, at worst, a ghost from her past. She did not view me as her daughter, but as a stranger. The stranger who had lived inside her body a half century before, a well-hidden secret.

Now, here I was, in the same position in which I'd lived inside her womb, curled into a ball, the sounds of a gutted animal that came from my mouth competing with a flood of my tears. I uncurled my tired bones and stretched my full, long length, and then I hoisted myself upright, thinking as I did that she had never seen me take my first steps, never heard my first word. Those moments were witnessed by a woman who had no use for me, a woman I learned to call "Mother," but almost as if it were her title.

Standing tall but feeling oh, so small, I lowered myself again to the floor and sat cross-legged on my meditation cushion. I watched the golden flame of my candles flicker brightly, and I was reminded of how things are constantly changing. I watched as the wick and the wax transformed with the heat of the fire, and I realized that I was changing, as well. I was not only changing in my mind, but in my flesh. I was changing cell by cell, just as my mother was changing cell by cell. We were both in a state of metamorphosis.

Nothing has been lost, I told myself, *and I am not afraid.*

But inside, I felt that I'd lost everything, and I was terrified to know that.

I got up and went into the kitchen and began to make a meal. It was a concrete chore and one I could assume readily, without having to think. Cutting vegetables and preparing dinner would keep me in the present. Paying attention to what I was doing would help keep the intruding emotions and thoughts at bay.

As I picked up each shockingly green bean to slice, I was mindful of each one's beauty. As I snipped off the stem ends with my razor-sharp paring knife, I was mindful of each motion. Staying mindful helps the mind to attend to what is really needed.

Each carrot was washed and sliced with care; the motions helped me to stay away from my unconscious anxieties and fears. I was comforted with each slice.

As I swirled the rice around in the water, I imagined each grain was a vessel for my pain.

I am here, I silently chanted. *I will survive.*

Had I known earlier that I carried a risk for lung disease, I could have acted differently. Would I have started smoking if I had known about her emphysema earlier? I had no idea, but it was too late. The damage to my lungs had been done. I was fighting for my life.

All my life, I had skipped the family history on my intake forms whenever I got any healthcare. Sitting in a doctor's office as they ask questions you have no answers for, is nothing but a reinforcement that you don't really exist. I had never known my genetic background, so I could do nothing about it, nor could I pass that information onto my daughter, for her own healthcare. My genetic history was an unknown, just as my future was.

Until, that is, I found my birth family. And when I did, and I discovered my mother had emphysema, I knew to pay closer attention to my own lungs. I had had lung problems since I was a child, including many episodes of bronchitis and pneumonia. When I complained of being short of breath, the doctors told me it was scarring. But once I knew there could be a genetic explanation for all my respiratory problems, I saw my doctor, who ordered a CT scan.

"So, what are the results? Is it emphysema?" I asked him, as if I were a nurse speaking of another patient.

"I'm afraid you have marked emphysema," he somberly told me. "You need to quit smoking immediately." Now that I realized the disturbing truth that like my own mother, my lungs were wearing out, I really knew things had to change with my health.

"Yup," I said, "I know. I will." And I would.

I had experienced many unusual illnesses and symptoms over the years, some life threatening. With the new diagnosis of emphysema, the time to take care of my health had arrived, so the first thing that I did was quit smoking. I had a suspicion that my other symptoms would soon form a pattern and that the puzzle would be solved through genetics.

The possibility that I was facing a shortened life really shook me up. My mother was already dying, and I didn't have much time left to become her daughter. Was I going to fly out one more time and have yet another awkward visit and then never see her again? Or was I going to claim my identity as my mother's daughter while I still had the time?

We traveled to Victoria several more times for visits, but they left me exhausted and slowly declining in health. I had a decision to make, and it was a difficult one. But the choice was clear. It was time to make a radical change. I had become ill enough to apply for disability pension. I wasn't sure what was going on with my health. I had planned on working for many years yet. Yet my body was failing in ways I hadn't seen before. If I was approved for disability, perhaps then I could move to British Columbia, while both my mother and I were still alive.

It would be my last chance to know my mother, to understand what had motivated her to give her own newborn to strangers. I knew that it would not be ideal. It would be hard and painful and insufficient. But I also knew that it was all I had, so when my disability claim was approved and my daughter decided she'd join me for a cross-country move, my decision was made. I'd move to Vancouver Island and get to know my mother before she died.

I stood in my empty house as the moving van pulled out of the driveway. My home, once full of things, had been whittled down to a few important belongings as I prepared for the journey of a lifetime. The chapters of my life had closed on the East Coast, and now new chapters awaited me on the West Coast. There would be family waiting, a mother waiting, a new life waiting. I was ready to cross the country to be with a total stranger as she left this earth, a stranger who had delivered me to this earth, and then left me on my own. I would find it in me to forgive and reconcile, no matter how limited that reconciliation might be.

But it wasn't long after we had established ourselves in our new lives that my mother's life began to leave her. She weakened with each passing day, and just as I had done with my adoptive mother, I came to her home with regularity, despite my own fatigue and growing physical distress. I sat with her and held her hand and comforted her. We went for drives when the days were good and on the bad ones, we sat, quietly, both in our own thoughts with the TV controlling the room.

We didn't talk much. The comfort that I found in my nursing role became a shield between us. She viewed me as a nurse, a woman who showed up each day to visit for a while, perhaps *the almost daughter.*

My siblings were her children. I would have to find the answers to my questions somewhere else. My mother had no answers to give me, but she could hold my hand, even if it was for only brief moments. I had a feeling she liked the hugs I gave her as I left for home and the soft whisper of "I love you," too.

Nine short months after I arrived, she was hospitalized. She would not be returning home. As I walked down the concrete hall of the palliative care ward where my mother lay dying, I smiled and said hello to the now-familiar faces of other families spending time with their loved ones in this last leg of their journey.

When I entered my mother's room, all heads turned toward me. A flash of relief moved over their faces, as if they had been waiting for the nurse to intervene in the care they couldn't provide. I would ease their worries; I would play that role. I studied the face of my sisters, the women who looked just like me. They were lost and confused, as they realized as I stood there, the sister/stranger/nurse, how little they knew of their mother. I was the sister who'd been concealed for a lifetime and had now returned as if a stark reminder that those we know most intimately harbor secrets of their own.

I turned to study the person in the hospital bed. She was resting quietly with medication to comfort her. My sisters were the ones in need of comfort.

"Let's go and have some dinner," I suggested.

We gathered quietly in the dining room, a shared space for the families of the palliative care unit, complete with kitchen and comfy couch and chairs. I leaned back in my chair, my exhaustion overtaking me as I watched the familiar scenes unfold around me. At a large table across from us, another family had gathered, their conversation animated and full of laughter. A birthday cake was brought in and I realized it was someone's birthday. I marveled at how in the midst of death, our days of birth still are cause for celebration.

My own birth was never celebrated. Sometimes I got shoes or something practical, like stationery so I could write my thank-you notes. One year, I got support hose.

I never got my wish.

I propped my elbows on the table and cradled my head in my hands. My eyelids were droopy with fatigue, yet my inner energy was brewing. I pushed my fingers into the corners of my eyes, trying to close the gates to my vision. They could open at any moment and release a flood of tears. As my fingers wandered over my face, I felt the bump of my nose. I smiled to myself as I looked over to my sisters and recognized the same nose on their faces. Such small pieces of my new identity were small miracles to me. To have never had any distinguishable genetic marker had been such a confusing element of my life. I had never "had my mother's eyes," or "my father's chin," as other children did. I was an anomaly. I became a chameleon trying to fit in, to belong somewhere. And now, with this bump on my nose that once distinguished me as "other," I was now included in one small way with this table full of girls.

"Let's stay the night here," I suggested to my sisters.

"Oh, okay, good plan," Laura agreed.

"Why? Do you think this is the night?" Carol asked, worried that her two nurse sisters felt it a good idea to stay.

"No, not yet," I said, "but she needs us near her."

Carol nodded, understanding the sacred space that dying creates within a family.

An imperfect, bent, and bandaged family, perhaps, but my family.

We informed the nurses of our decision, and they returned with the things we'd need: blankets, pillows, cots. As the three of us decided who would sleep where and on what, I was suddenly struck by the overwhelming presence of three. Three sisters and a mother.

For me, so many years of missed nighttime conversations full of whispers and giggles. I thought about the squabbles I'd missed, the daily conflicts that create a family history and memories that bind the family together.

And I suddenly was overwhelmed with heavy sadness. I was sad to realize that it wasn't until our mother lay dying that we were finally together to sleep by her bedside for the first time ever. The room was lit by one small nightlight that cast shadows in long, slender fingers that danced over our beds and cots and the forms we made laying on them. In the background came the music that I had brought to play—soft, soothing music to calm our screaming nerves. One by one, the mellow notes slipped out of the music box and surrounded us with gentle song, while an orchestra of hospital notes wrote a different song in the dark air.

Sounds of oxygen hissing through skinny plastic tubing.

Breaths being sucked in desperation with each puff of air.

Whispers of three sisters and a giggle thrown in for balance.

Silence. The silence of grief and pending death.

Rustles of sheets and sighs of despair and fatigue completed the orchestra.

Together, they danced in a song of a life ending and a family beginning.

Gradually, the night rhythms flowed together into a soothing melody. The breathing patterns that enveloped me deepened and became a sweet song of sleep, turning my mother's labored breathing into a rhythmic backbeat. As I lay on the hospital cot, listening to her breathe, I knew that her death was not an ending, but a transformation of energy. Matter always becomes energy, and her energy would become a part of us, surrounding all of us throughout our lives.

I felt comforted by my realization and thought of the Buddhist poem that says we are not caught within this body, but are life without boundaries. We have never been born and will never have to die. Birth and death are only a door through which we go in and out, a game of hide and seek where we will one day meet again at the true source.

If only I could shake off the trauma of my birth to fully embrace what I knew to be true—that my birth was a mere blip on the universal screen of life.

I had been telling my mother the Buddhist teachings in our quiet time together. She never commented on them, but she would always smile. I thought of her gentle, understanding smile as I lay in the hospital room, listening to my family breathe around me. Peace laid its fuzzy blanket over the darkened room, but my eyes refused to give up their watch. They remained focused on the person in the bed beside me, *My mother.* I drank in the essence of her, trying to fill those thirsty places that had waited so long for nourishment. There was little time left to spare. She would soon move on to another realm, and I would have to be satisfied with the crumbs leftover from the years gone by. The half-century we were apart.

"You should be grateful we took you," my adoptive mother would tell me. "Nobody else wanted you." I learned to be grateful for the crumbs of recognition and affection she offered, and I scooped them up greedily, as if they were diamonds she had tossed across the floor.

Unfolding my legs of lead, I got off the cot and moved quietly to the chair beside her head. The plastic was cold, like the floor beneath my bare feet, but the cold helped me to stay alert so I could watch over my mother a little bit longer. The nightlight created dark hollows in her cheeks, and her sunken eyes struggled to open as her dreams played on behind her closed lids. I watched as her weak fingers twitched, as if they wanted to be held. My hand reached out, as if offering her my heart in my open palm. My hand enveloped hers as her eyelids opened wide. Our eyes searched for the words hidden in each other's gaze and found comfort. No words were needed.

I sent her my peace, my acceptance, and my love straight from my heart, as if it were traveling through my veins, out through my fingertips, and into her. A heat so profound it startled us both emanated from our hands. The heat spread across our flesh where it touched, skin to skin, and I tensed as she looked at me as if wanting more. In unison, we sucked in the experience and reveled in the warmth, before it passed as quickly as it had come. I got up from the chair and lay, as quietly as I could, back on my cot.

I must have fallen asleep, because suddenly the hall lights flashed on, and another early morning began. Our moment together was over. My feet slid off the side of the bed and hit the cold floor with surprise. My toes wiggled around in circles trying to get used to the feeling. I wished it were earth I was touching, so that my toes could grip the planet and I could hang on for dear life. I let my feet relax into the icy floor and the coolness traveled upward, sending chills through every pore and fiber.

I'd been awake most of the night, and the heaviness of fatigue gripped the parts of my body that should have moved freely but instead refused to oblige me. My sisters were stirring on their cots, trying to make sense of where they were and what was going on as the noise of the hospital turned from a background lull to a loud cacophony of morning clamor.

I realized I had to get dressed and turn back into the nurse that I was, before their sleep-filled minds became more alert. *The almost daughter* that I had been through the night knew it was time to go, to return to my safe role as a nurse so that the "real" daughters would not feel trespassed upon. They didn't tell me I didn't belong, of course, but it was a discomforting truth that we all silently accepted.

Breakfast trays arrived for patients who didn't want to eat, and liquids were hung on poles for those who were not thirsty. It was the life inside the hospital walls that I knew so well from years of working inside them. Impermanence becomes permanent in the hospital, where everything changes and nothing remains. Understanding such inconstancy helps the suffering to find their peace. I inhaled deeply to find my own.

A gasping struggle for air shattered my thoughts, and we all rushed to surround the body holding the diseased lungs that were fighting for breath. One daughter sat her up. Another daughter rubbed her back. The "almost daughter" went for the nurse.

The panic of not being able to breathe is terrifying. Watching your mother slowly suffocate is even more so.

A nurse rushed in carrying a magical drug. Within seconds, her struggle to breathe had eased and air entered the flaccid pockets of tissue of my mother's oxygen-starved cells. Another crisis had ended.

I watched as my sisters surrounded our mother and knew it was time to slip off. I needed to find a safe place, to step out of my nursing role.

"I'll be back soon," I told them, as they nodded in agreement their good-byes. With all my effort, I moved foot by foot in the direction of my car. Each step took energy I didn't have and felt heavier with each footfall. The pit of my belly was full and heavy with dread—dread for the inevitable. Dread for what the day would bring.

As I pulled open the car door and climbed into my alone place, I exhaled the night's worries. Hospital air filled with the energy of death escaped my own damaged lungs and steamed my already foggy windows. I was safe in my alone place, encased in my metal car house. I rested my head against the steering wheel, secure in the knowledge that no one could see me. People become invisible when they step inside their cars. People notice the cars, not the people inside them.

My fingers resisted turning the key that would begin my day's journey. I relished the peaceful feeling I had sitting in a cocoon of silence and mist, the same silence and mist I'd once, so very long ago, discovered in the mountains as I watched a herd of wild horses.

As the motor came on and the car filled with my breath, the cocoon spell began to break. I watched the mist outside the car and remembered Dali, the mare who led the wild horses, and the miraculous vision of watching her and her family emerge from a mist that seemed to lift from the earth toward the heavens.

Watching the mist swirl outside my cocoon car, I knew one thing to be true. Something was going to happen.

If you look deeply into the palm of your hand,
You will see your parents and all generations of your ancestors.
All of them are alive in this moment. Each is present in your body.
You are the continuation of each of these people.
—Thich Nhat Hanh

Chapter 16

The End of the Beginning

As I worked my way through my daily chores, my thoughts wandered back to the hospital. There was so much that I just didn't understand. Who were these people who were my family? What was really going on in my mother's mind and heart? Why did she have to be so close to death, now that I'd finally found her?

I forced the thoughts out of my head and willed myself to focus on the present. The grief and loss that had come to define my life swept through me like the tides, their ebb and flow washing tears across my face like gentle waves.

Occasionally, when my eyes were closed in silence, I could see my Wall of Secrets. I wished I still had the actual cabinet of drawers, something I could actually see and feel and open and close, but all I had left, since my mother sold it, were my memories. But they were enough. It was enough to conjure the image of the Wall of Secrets, where I could put my suffering away, close it in a drawer to be forgotten.

So many secrets had accumulated in its drawers, secrets waiting to be sorted and dumped into the ocean, where they'd be taken out to sea. Whenever I tossed out a secret like that, it would instantly dissolve as if it had never been in the first place.

Knowing what I'd held so tightly in those drawers was the clue I had been looking for in emptying forever the secrets held in trust. It wasn't any one secret that I was rummaging for in my mind. The secret key had always been there, and it was so simple. All I needed was to look beneath the layers of pain, as if peeling an onion, to expose the truth.

The truth was that I didn't need the secrets I'd stuffed in there. The truth was that I needed those drawers to be emptied, before I could make room for something other than my pain. I needed to empty those drawers of secrets to fill them with my family, with my identity. With the answers to the questions that I'd sought all these years. It was time to empty those drawers.

And it was time to return to the hospital. An invasion of emotion surged through my body as a sense of unrest and hesitancy mixed with the soup of sadness that was simmering in my soul. Each part of me had to be independently instructed to move, as I forced first one leg, then another, to proceed toward the door. It was as if there were forces beyond my awareness that were acting upon me, forcing me to move, forcing me to stand still.

As I reached my car, I paused to look toward the eastern sky. In the distance, I saw the outlines of mountains topped with ice-cream peaks, still unmelted from the long, cold winter. My muscles were coiled like tightly wound springs, and as I inhaled the ocean air, they relaxed and pulled me into the waiting car. I sat quietly, focusing on my breath, knowing that my mother was struggling to find hers, desperately struggling to keep breathing so that she could stay alive.

Breathing in and out, I circulated the fresh ocean air and energy until it reached my weary cells. My mind cleared and my body calmed as the tension I was holding in was released. And with it went all my negativities, my sadness, and my pain.

I'm ready, I told myself. *I'm ready to return to her.*

When I left my mother's bedside, I hadn't expected to have such difficulty returning, but something inside me had a powerful grip on me, as if I knew that this would not be an ordinary day. But I had to return; there was no other choice.

I turned the key in the ignition and let the car drive me there, my hands merely steering the wheel. Leaving the glorious mountains and the safety of my home, I returned to the land of concrete and predictability. But I hadn't gone more than twenty feet inside the concrete hall when I sensed a different energy than there had been when I'd left.

Each footstep took me closer to the center of change. The energy grew darker and heavier until I finally reached my mother's room. Walking inside, I knew something terribly dark was in the air. The room was static with death rays that overshadowed the sun, and the faces that turned toward me were lined with worry and fear. They were seeking answers from me, to questions they left unspoken.

I forced my lips into a curl, a suggestion of a smile. It wasn't a smile of joy, but of pleasantry, as if to say, "It's going to be all right." But I wasn't so sure it would be.

"She's not doing well," Carol said. "She's really struggling.

"Yes, I see that," I said. My fingers wrapped themselves around her exposed toes at the end of the bed. Her toes were cold, icy cold, and bluish in color. I knew that sign well. It meant that her circulation was going to the place that needed it the most: her heart. Life always returns to the heart.

"You need to stay now," I told them. Those five words said all that was needed.

Family members gathered around my mother's bed to say goodbye. All bore tears of sadness and memories of their history of love. I sat to the side, in a different place of grief. As my siblings were grieving for the memories they had, I was grieving for the memories I never experienced and lost in time forever.

My mother's eyes were closed, and we surrounded her bedside as her lifeblood slowed and settled. When it no longer flowed, her spirit was set free, and we were, all of us, left without a mother.

Amidst the overwhelming sadness, a wave of peace crept in. My mother was gone, but I had, however imperfectly, known her. Held her. And been there when she left this world, just as she had been there when I had entered it.

Driving home along the ocean shore, I watched the evening fog roll in. I welcomed the blanket of soft gray and the protection and comfort it offered. My mother's family had gathered at her home, but I did not join them. I had no memories to share, and I could not share in their loss, for mine was something different, something that would not be understood, and yet I yearned for their presence, their closeness, their love and support. But I grieved alone.

With my car parked, I again took a moment to collect my thoughts and found the center where I felt most grounded with myself. Entering my home, I sunk into my couch and relaxed into my own isolation. With my pointer finger, I traced the flower pattern in the nubby upholstery on the couch, and automatically, my childhood mantra fluttered from my lips.

"I'm safe. I'm safe. I'm safe ..."

In the morning, I awoke without a mother. Another day was on the horizon, and the outside air was cool and moist. The mountains were hidden behind the mask of fog, but I knew they were there, surrounding and protecting me. I paused at the window and gazed across the frosty ocean; I watched for any morning activity, but I saw only the activity of the natural world. The clouds were unmoving in the shimmering sunrise. An eagle cruised the waterfront, looking for breakfast.

They say that if you see an eagle, your prayers are taken to heaven, because the eagle flies higher than any other bird. They fly above the storm.

I wondered if that eagle knew my prayers.

As I stood there, watching the motherless sky that now cradled me, I saw that life continues on with the rhythms of nature turning its pages. And I felt an astounding sense of tender calm.

A loud ringing startled me back to my inside world.

"You should come over soon," Carol said on the other end of the phone.

"Sure," I said hesitantly. I felt like an intruder into another family's grief and didn't want to go. But I would; I knew I had to.

I completed my morning activities, all the while trying to focus on what I was doing and not let my mind wander to my mother's death or the past that I'd never had with her or the future I'd never have with her. I had to stay present, but I kept slipping back into my past. A layer of dusty sadness covered me, and even in the shower, I couldn't scrub it off. My tears fell and merged with the water, and then they slid into the drain, where they were gone but not forgotten.

I briskly scrubbed my body dry to erase any signs of distress. I was so confused about my place in this new motherless family. With my mother alive, I had a reason to be among them, but with her dead, what was my role? Would they close the door on me once and for all? Had they seen me only as their mother's secret, *her almost daughter,* or perhaps as the nurse? Had I clung too closely to that role?

It was the only role I felt safe in, the nurse's role. Who would I be without my mother? Did I still belong? Would they still want me around?

"Be still … be still … be still," I said out loud. I took one long breath at a time, inhaling and exhaling with purpose because that was all I could manage. Another new chapter in my life was beginning and I didn't know what the opening sentence would be, much less the ending.

It was so difficult to be mindful of each moment. There was so much confusion within my chattering mind and such an empty place inside my heart. As I drove across town to enter the unfamiliar family world, I felt my anxiety building.

"Breathe; breathe; breathe," I said to myself, again out loud, as I drove across the city. When I reached Carol's house, I saw that everyone was sitting outside on the deck, drinking coffee. Hugs were traded between everyone, and the "how-are-you doings" were asked. The sisters beckoned me to sit between them.

Glances were passed back and forth between them that I didn't understand and clearly wasn't part of. My anxiety turned to paranoia as my sense of exclusion intensified. What had they been talking about before I'd gotten there? What was their plan for me? Which of them had been selected to give me my farewell lecture?

"You tell her," Laura said.

"No, you tell her," Carol echoed.

"Tell me what?" I asked nervously, not wanting to hear the answer. I never should have come; I should have stayed safe in my comforting home.

Carol took the lead. "Last night, we were talking," she said, and I stiffened, "about mom's rings."

I forced the roaring in my ears to quiet so I could hear what she had to say.

Her words, which had been entering my ears in bits and pieces, began to roll into sentences.

"We know she had three. There was this antique one, this sapphire, and the family ring." Each sister held out a hand to show me her new ring.

"The antique one was perfect for Laura," Carol said, "and I like the sapphire." I saw the dazzling, beautiful rings on their hands and wondered about the stories each ring had to tell. "And the family one is for you."

The words hung in the air, suspended by my shock. I looked back and forth between them, not quite understanding. But Carol continued.

"All these years, we used to ask Mom about the stones. She always told us there was a stone for each of us, and one for her. But that never really made any sense because then she had two for herself—a diamond and a sapphire."

Then, in unison, Carol and Laura both said, "But we never knew about you."

I struggled to grasp what they were trying to tell me. Everyone was watching, and my belly was tied into knots of emotion. My mind was scrambling to put the words into some kind of order that would make sense and explain the building excitement.

"Look, look, don't you see?" Laura said, pointing to the ring.

"No, see what?" I said, still confused.

"It's your birthstone!" cried Laura. "Yours and Mom's are the same, so she could say it was for her, but she has the diamond in the middle. It's your stone; she had it set for you. She had always wanted you in there, too."

I stared at the ring I was holding. "Are you just telling me this to make me feel better?" I asked between my tears, as I began to sob.

"Of course not," Laura said. "Why would we do that? This ring is for you. We want you to have it."

I wiggled the ring on my finger and stared in disbelief. "Thank you ... thank you ... thank you," I said softly as I caressed the different stones. It was all too much for me to comprehend.

I turned it and touched it and stared at it. It was a simple but beautiful ring of gems and gold, and a reminder for all my life of all that I had lost, and a lesson in all that must be found.

The moment you completely accept your non-peace,
Your non-peace becomes transmuted into peace.
Anything you accept fully will take you into peace.
This is the miracle of surrender.
—Eckhart Tolle

Chapter 17

Into the Mist

Once again, I found myself at the airport, only this time I was flying with my sisters. We were taking a container that held my birth mother, *their mother*, back to her special place, the place where she rode her horses.

I would have given anything to have been able to ride my horse beside hers, to experience that bond between mother and daughter, between humans and horses. It was painful to think of all the possibilities that could have been, the possibilities that would never become realities. I had been part of many kinds of families over the years and had never found one that really fit, except when I was with horses.

"Are you ready yet? Should we go now?" The voice broke my silent world of internal reflection. It was Carol, the oldest sister—well, the oldest until I arrived—and she had the typical take-charge attitude of a firstborn. She had made the arrangements for the memorial tea in Alberta and was anxious to get on with it. I remained seated in the boarding area and watched as the passengers snaked in line to board, maneuvered their carry-on baggage onto their shoulders and backs, and handed over their boarding passes for inspection.

I felt the telltale signs of my own stress emerging: the hot prickles, the flush, the flags of warning standing at attention on my arms. I tried to ease into a relaxed state so that no one would notice my growing anxiety. I closed my eyes and fixed my mind on a distant lake from my past, a lake cradled in the mountains, where my wild-horse family rested and fed. I thought of the diamonds twinkling on the lake's surface, imaging them so clearly it was as if the lake itself was smiling at me, beckoning me to return. I felt the mist that had enveloped me that memorable morning so many years before and the early-morning dampness of my sleep sack. Most of all, I recalled the soft horse conversations that drifted through the mist and wrapped my ears in a soft, velvety embrace. For the first time in my life, I had felt accepted. I belonged. I was home.

"Claire! Snap out of it! We have to get on the plane now!" With a flip of a hand, her long, blonde hair snapped over Laura's shoulder, and the harsh note in her tone brought me to attention. Carol, always the responsible one, carried the urn gingerly, so gently and lovingly, yet with the slightest hint of fear. I listened to the sisters argue back and forth. Who should carry her? Where should she sit?

Inside my head, I was screaming. *Don't you get it? Don't you see? She's left already! Those are just ashes, for Christ's sake!*

For them, their mother was hidden inside the wooden box they carried, but for me, the box was empty and held only ashes. Watching them, I realized I wasn't one of them. I wasn't really participating in this ritual but observing it as an onlooker.

A couple of hours later, we'd arrived in Alberta. My role was assigned: I would be the driver, charged with delivering the sisters safely to their mother's memorial and the awaiting family. The hairs on my arms stood erect, like bristles on a brush, and shivers ran up and down my spine as if screaming in horror. I rubbed my hands up and down my arms, trying to warm them, to brush the bristly hairs back down and settle my panic, but all that changed was that my ears began to burn hot and red. *The lake ... think of the lake ... so cool and icy ... as I wade in through the glittering diamond skin and marvel at its velveteen smoothness ... oh, so cool ...*

I drove silently, the sisters bantering back and forth in a steady buzz in the background of my mind. I pictured myself floating, becoming one with the water. I pictured myself home, resting on Mother Earth's waterbed, safe and content. In the background, I caught bits of history being tossed around with an element of no importance. To them, it was just the past, but to me, every detail was new and of great importance. I had no history with my birth mother or my siblings, so every detail they revealed about their past was a huge discovery of my heritage.

Don't they get it? I wondered. Of course they didn't. They couldn't. They were grieving. They had no experience with being relinquished by their mother to be raised by an abusive stranger, so they couldn't possibly grasp the feelings going through me at that moment. They could, of course, sympathize, even empathize, but they could not really know my past, any more than I could know theirs.

I understood all that, but at the same time, it separated us. I was alone in my journey to my mother's final resting place. The chatter about old boyfriends and parties and Christmases past stirred an unrelenting sadness inside me. They were remembering all the things I was not a part of, had never experienced, and so I had no memories to share. I winced and sucked in my breath and then made a little snort, like a horse.

It was Heart Horse.

I thought of Heart Horse, an imaginary horse that I held in my heart most of my life; Heart Horse protected me when others would not, listened to me when others turned away, shared my sorrows and fears and joys when I was all alone. Heart Horse was once again in my heart, trying to get my attention.

I wanted to tell my sisters about Heart Horse, but I didn't dare. I wasn't sure if they would understand my stories about Heart Horse, that wild, unpredictable creature that had been such a huge part of my life. He was there, when they were not. He knew the pain I'd experienced throughout my life; he had felt it, but they had not. They had no idea what my life had been. But Heart Horse understood.

And Heart Horse understood that as I drove to my birth mother's memorial, I was terrified. Terrified of facing the finality of her death. Terrified of facing the uncertainty of my future with my siblings. Terrified of meeting the rest of the family who would be waiting: the cousins, the in-laws, and the friends who had known my mother all the years I had not.

But what I was most terrified of was that nobody even knew that I existed. I'd had that fear for some time, and I wasn't sure when or where it had started, but from little comments that had been made or the way in which certain topics were dropped or shifted, I came to sense that even though I'd found them three years before and had lived on the Island for almost a year, I was still a secret. I was still the family shame that was buried in secrets and lies. And that hurt so deeply that my hurt was turning to fear—fear that I was right.

The feeling of not mattering, of not belonging, of nonexistence, had come to take over my life and identity for so long that it seemed as if it were a part of my cells, as much a part of me as my DNA. It was a cellular belief that had taken root deep inside my soul.

As these thoughts scampered through my conscious mind, they grew more powerful, until I found myself thinking of only one thing: I was invisible. I was going to say good-bye to a mother who had said good-bye to me more than a half a century before. And after all these years, I was just a ghost child—an invisible child that no one could see because no one even knew I'd ever happened.

My fingers gripped the steering wheel until my knuckles were white, as my eyes stared straight ahead. In the hospital, I played the role of nurse. In the car, I played the role of driver. What role was I going to play when I stepped out of the car? The stranger? I couldn't play the role of daughter, nor sibling, nor cousin; those roles had already been taken. I was the secret.

Maybe that would be my role.

We had arrived. It reminded me of when I first landed in Victoria and couldn't get off the plane because I was so paralyzed by fear. That same fear held me fast in my seat once again.

"Mom? Come on, Mom, get out," my daughter said. She had flown in from Toronto, once again playing her own role, as she opened the door to the driver's seat and motioned for me to get moving.

I planted my feet firmly on the dusty road, reconnecting myself to Mother Earth. She always grounded me and helped me feel safe.

I felt Heart Horse; he had been quiet for so long and was now suddenly flailing around, his sharp little hooves digging into my sides like a child I carried inside me. It was a warning; I knew that much. But what he was warning me about, I didn't know. There was no real reason I should have been so frightened. After all, regardless of the circumstances, this was my family, however imperfectly defined. It shouldn't be so frightening or cause me such distress. No one was doing, or failing to do, anything to account for my anxiety.

But I couldn't shake the fact that it was there, overwhelming and paralyzing me with every step I took.

As we approached the crowd, I fell back and hid myself in the background. As my sisters bustled around, setting tables and organizing chairs, they caught up on gossip and news from their aunt and cousins, the family that had known about me while my siblings did not. I watched them, like a voyeur, not knowing how to merge. No one introduced me, and the longer I remained in the background, the more my fear began to grow.

They don't want to introduce me! They're as frightened as I am! I convinced myself that they were avoiding the elephant in the room, the identity of the stranger they'd brought along to the memorial, as if I were unreal.

I watched as more and more people arrived, their chatter and laughter and hugs passed among my sisters and brother and their families. Condolences were passed out like chocolates that weren't offered to me. I stood alone, apart from the crowd, and busied myself with unloading coolers, as if I were the caterer. Maybe that was my role.

Eventually, a sister glided up to me and pulled me toward the chairs that were filled with old ladies dressed in sun hats, costume jewelry, and practical shoes. My feet seemed to be glued to the floor, and she practically had to uproot me from the spot I'd planted myself on.

"Come on," Carol said, "I want you to meet some of my mom's good friends."

I gathered up all my courage, took a deep breath, and put on my most pleasant smile.

"Mrs. Bates," Carol said, "this is my new sister, Claire. Mom gave her up for adoption and she just found us!"

I extended my hand in greeting as the old woman looked at me in horror and turned her head away.

She didn't know. She was my mother's good friend, but she never knew. For all those years, her friend had kept such a secret from her. I was stunned.

I wasn't so stunned that she didn't know I'd been born, though that was bad enough. But she didn't even know now, after I'd returned to my mother's life. My fears weren't unfounded after all. I really was a secret.

I couldn't understand how after all those years, I still was a family shame. I still did not exist in their social world. I was an embarrassment, the secret that nobody told. Heart Horse gave me a good kick and began to gallop wildly, my invisible friend there to share my pain and fear and offer what comfort he could provide.

Droplets of sweat began to dribble down the sides of my face like tears. I was unable to push or pull any words out past my lips to respond to anything. As I wiped my brow, my hand caught a flood of warm fluid, and I knew it wasn't my sweat. I was crying. The saltwater trickled across my mouth and I caught the salty taste with my tongue.

"Damn," I said out loud. The old woman's eyes flashed at mine, as if I'd just given her the evidence she needed to judge me as something bad. Something to explain the deceit her friend had perpetrated on her all those years. She looked at me, as if waiting for me to offer some further explanation for my existence, but all she saw were my tears. For fifty years, they hadn't sprung from my eyes, but suddenly, it was as if my face needed them to survive. I pushed them back with my hand, trying to stop the flow.

Pulling my hand from Carol's grip, I barely missed her long fingers, which were grasping to hold on. I gave a quick glance to make sure my daughter was okay, and after a quick view of the scene around me, I spotted her. She gave me a smile and a quick wave, enough to let me know she was okay and give me permission to do what I had to do.

With a forced smile, I nodded back and headed for the door. If there were any calls for me to come back, I didn't hear them; I forced myself to ignore them, because I couldn't bear the thought that no one would even notice I was leaving.

Five big steps and I was out the door, out to fresh air at last. And freedom.

I'm free. I'm free. I'm free. I repeated the words to myself again and again as the warm Alberta air caressed my face and dried the salty drops as they continued to slide down my face. Heart Horse gave a little gallop forward; he was also thrilled to be free of the restraints that had us both tightly in its grips. I knew it was time to set Heart Horse free once again, now that we were out in the great Alberta wild, but I wanted to hold him in my imagination a moment longer, until I knew that I was truly safe from the pain and fear.

The sounds of nature beckoned me. The only reality I knew at that instant was the ground I stood upon: the earth, the sky, the water, and the animals I loved and trusted to love me in return.

I brushed away any remaining tears and ventured forth. I heard the musical sound of a creek ahead and listened to it bouncing over shiny rocks and tumbling in a rhapsody of sound. The music called me, as it always did, to come closer. I glanced back to see if anyone was watching or noticing I was missing, but I saw only a group of people all connected to each other, telling funny stories of the past that I wasn't part of. I had the urge to run, to hide, to escape from the crowd that wasn't pursuing me, but I knew it wasn't necessary. There was no urgency.

I moved quickly in the direction of a little bridge I spotted in the distance. As the distance grew greater between the grieving family and me, I thought I heard my name called, but I was sure it was just my imagination.

Don't look back. Don't look back. Don't look back. I forced myself to look forward and not turn back to the crowd that ignored me. I quickened my steps, and only when I was on the safety of the wooden bridge poised between the river's banks did I chance another glance back. It wasn't my imagination. Laura was sitting on a bench with a friend, having a cigarette and waving frantically. Her long, blonde hair swished back and forth like a fluttering flag as she tried to catch my attention.

Was it a good-bye wave or a come-here wave? I had no idea. If it was a good-bye wave and I came back, I'd look pathetic. On the other hand, if it was a come-here wave and I turned away, I'd look rude.

The only thing to do was pretend I didn't see it so I wouldn't have to make a bad decision. I stood on the bridge, feeling solid, its warm, wooden slats bending beneath my feet, as if any moment they might break and I'd fall into the river and drown.

Which somehow made me feel safe at last.

Stopping for a moment, I admired the greens and blues of the bubbling water as it made its orchestrated dance down the rocks. A sunray caught a tiny bubble and it glittered just like the long-ago diamonds on the mountain lake, where I'd watched the wild horses graze.

Breathe in. Breathe out. Breathe in.

I'm safe. I'm safe. I'm safe.

Memories flooded my heart and soul just like the bubbling water I was watching. It caught me off guard, and I needed a moment to reflect on all that was happening. I sucked in the country air, inhaling deeply so that I could absorb all its nutrients and energy.

My feet took me over the bridge and down a dusty path that led to a fence. I loved to touch things, especially wooden things, and the urge to do so grew irresistible. My fingers reached out eagerly to caress the splintered logs. For years, this log had had the job of keeping something in the field, or perhaps, keeping something out of it. My fingers landed in a hole that had once had a wood knot shaped in a perfect circle. My finger traced the outline of the circle, stimulating the memory of the buttons on my dad's old, leather chair. So many times I had hidden behind that chair in the library, circling those buttons and saying my mantras.

I'm safe. I'm safe. I'm safe.

With my eyes closed, I watched a movie of those years play itself out, secret by secret, and I wondered why those memories were flooding me at that particular moment—perhaps because I was so aware of my tenuous role as a daughter.

If I were a good daughter, I realized, I would be back with the others, consoling them, laughing with them, and reminiscing about the few memories I'd shared with my birth mother. But in reality, I was no one's daughter. Not my birth mother's, nor my adoptive parents', who had wished me dead and cast me out.

I closed my eyes and let the movie of my past play inside my head; my eyelids turned into a screen on which my life history was projected.

Suddenly, my lids snapped open with the recognition of something terribly familiar. It was the smells and the sounds softly playing in the distance. *Yes! Yes! Yes!* I could hear it! It was a horse conversation. In the very field on the other side of the fence where I stood, there were horses.

My feet took charge and my legs followed, without question, one foot up and over and the other one right behind. Only three wooden rails held me back, but they wouldn't for long. I hoisted my leg up and over the rail, and as my body twisted, the other leg came with it until I was inside the fence completely. I stopped briefly just to make sure that I hadn't been seen. I looked back at the crowd gathered for the memorial. They had shrunk until they were barely recognizable, but I could tell that the hall was still swollen with people and conversation. Even from a distance, I could see the air swell to accommodate them all, the hall itself trying to expand to make room for all the stories being told and all the secrets being kept. I had a momentary vision of the hall actually exploding, spewing forth funeral folk for miles and miles, to be lost along with all their secrets.

I grinned diabolically at the thought, then realized just as I did that my pants had been caught on the rail, and I practically ripped them off as I tried to step away from the fence. My grin turned sheepish as I realized the irony of my near miss. *So much for wishing them disaster,* I thought. *It nearly brought me a social disaster of my own.* The thought of returning to the group with my pants ripped off my legs made me chuckle at my own self-inflicted embarrassment.

But my thoughts turned more serious when I realized I couldn't untangle myself from the fencing. My pant leg was still stuck fast to the rail, and with a pull of annoyance, I yanked my pant leg, only to hear the sound of material ripping.

Well, at least they were still on me. But they didn't look good.

I could just imagine the conversation.

Well, we knew she didn't belong anyway.

What was she thinking?

No proper daughter would be out in the field in her good clothes.

No wonder Marilyn gave her away.

I didn't know why I was thinking these things; no one had done or said anything to suggest that this is how they thought. But it was how I thought. It had been drilled into my head again and again with my mother's taunts.

Child of Satan's blood.

We can send you back.

Why didn't you just die?

I forced myself to shift my thinking of the past to attention to the present. The dry stubble beneath my feet was crispy, and it flattened with each step. Ahead, I saw green, and behind me, water music played. And far beyond, I heard the horses, deep in conversation.

I desperately wanted to take off my shoes, to enjoy the sensations beneath my feet, but that would only sidetrack me. Behind me, the hall breathed in and out, full of everything I knew nothing about: the history, the emotions, the family, the stories, the secrets—they were discussing everything and nothing.

Because I was the secret, and I was gone.

I found the perfect spot, soft and warm with a touch of dark earth showing through the evergreen blades. My body folded itself into the blades of grass, and I immediately felt as if I were home and connected to something. My body was exhausted, and my eyelids were heavy. I felt as if I'd carried the weight of the world on my back in my short walk into the field, and had finally, just that moment, set it down.

My arms reached out to touch the earth and the delicate evergreen blades that felt like silken feathers on the brown earth's firm, moist body.

I'm okay now. I'm okay now. I'm okay now.

I'm okay; I'm okay; I'm okay.

My eyes relaxed as I closed my lids and watched my memories of the wild horses I'd once known. It had been decades since that day in the mountains, and so much had changed in my life, yet this singular memory returned again and again, and I didn't know why I clung to it so. Why did the memory always resurface? What did it mean?

I remembered Dali, the guardian mare who'd reigned over the herd, and smiled. Every time I saw a brown-splattered horse, I believed for a second it was Dali. But I knew in my heart, it wasn't. I knew that somewhere in the wild mountains, she was galloping, watching, guarding, protecting. And it always brought me peace to know that she was still wild, and still free. A beautiful creature like that should never be captured and restrained.

The energy from the earth began to penetrate my skin and fill me with its warmth. I felt such pure joy and perfection, a sense of belonging to my Mother Earth. I could again smell the wildflowers I'd once smelled when I gazed upon the wild horses, and I recalled how brilliantly purple they were as they bowed in the wind over the diamond lake. I smelled the ripe apple juice as it dripped over my fingers after waiting with my arm outstretched for hours in the sun, making my offering to Dali. I could feel the ground shiver as the horses in my memory thundered off to return to the tree line and mountains from where they'd emerged that misty morning.

When I opened my eyes, they were there. The horses. I knew that they would come. I had felt it. I sat up ever so slowly, so that I would not startle them. I was surprised that I'd remembered the rules—the rules for wild horses, except these weren't wild, of course. I closed my eyes and breathed in their energy, that wonderful horse energy. I was acutely aware of a new kind of heat—horse heat. And horse breath. Their snorts and snuffles assured me of their closeness.

Right before me stood a mare with the identical markings of Dali, my Dali. This wasn't a memory or fantasy; it was a slice of reality that had shattered my daydreams as it plunged itself into my fantasies like a blaze of bright light in the depths of darkness.

Of course I knew the horse could not possibly be Dali, but the identical markings were astounding. It was as if she had magically returned to me in this new, un-aged horse's body.

Lost in my thoughts, I felt the new Dali's presence. Her warm breath and soft lips reached toward me for nuzzling. At once, a river of tears fell from my eyes, as I knew I was finally, truly home. All those years of searching were finally over. I was home, on this earth, where I belonged, a child of the universe, and yet sadly, as the almost daughter.

Epilogue

Eight years have passed since I sat in that field with the horses on that day of loss. Many lessons have been learned, secrets discovered, genetics studied, layers uncovered since then.

There are core belief systems that are hardwired into an adoptee's brain. Buried deep within the limbic system lays the tangled web of the neurons responsible for so many of our daily emotions. They are filled with hidden secrets, details of our coping skills, beliefs, and awareness pre-birth.

Everyone, adopted or not, suffers from similar feelings that adoptees feel so profoundly. Feelings of not belonging, abandonment, loss, unworthiness, and grief are a normal part of life. A person raised by her genetic family, however, has roots to keep her strong in the belief, the knowing, that underneath it all, she is loved and belongs to a family. She exists. For adoptees, the experiences of self and our origins are profoundly different. There are no roots to hold us firm. No family to hold us close.

Many books have been written and research has been published that documents in-utero babies beginning to learn and know their mother intimately. From reactions to sounds and the energetic vibrations of love, it's all felt in the womb. Already, in utero, adoptees know and feel the stress of not being wanted. When babies are removed and placed into a strange environment, those ingrained belief systems and coping mechanisms that are already hardwired begin to protect from the effects of loss, the Primal Wound. This manifests in a sense of loss, basic mistrust, a loss of sense of self, self- esteem, and self-worth throughout life.

The Primal Wound should not be about blame and guilt; it should be about understanding. There are no X-rays for hearts and souls, only brave adoptees willing to put their stories out into the world to educate others of the reality of adoption.

Adopted persons need to integrate the wound of separation to become fully authentic individuals. We so badly need time and empathy; they are things we thirst for. Unfortunately, for many of us, that crater of emptiness will never be filled due to a lack of understanding. Until our craters are filled with love and understanding and empathy, we will not be able to move forward in integration and change.

I can only speak of my experience, and that has been a lifetime of searching, as I wrote about in my first memoir, *Finding Heart Horse*. I didn't fit or belong anywhere. In fact, subconsciously, most of us who have been adopted feel we don't really exist. I know that sounds strange when you can physically see that you do, but somewhere in our twisted neurons is a feeling of nonbeing, nonexistence.

Grief surrounds an adopted person with an aura of sadness and detachment, which may mystify others. You put on your masks for the world, but people sense that bubble of protection. Sadness shows in our eyes.

Some would say we live in duality. There is the face we put on for society and then there is that unknown, dark, mysterious place that has no history, no genetic information, nobody we look like, no evidence to prove we came from somewhere. It isn't until we search for our biological roots that we actually get to the core layer that will expose those defense mechanisms that have allowed us to survive. That process is called "coming out of the fog" by adoptees.

I have functioned, as many of my peers have, as a divided self. R. D. Laing called it the True Self and False Self. Betty Jean Lifton put it into an adoptee's context. She called it the Artificial Self and the Forbidden Self, neither of which is completely true or false.

As a child, one believes his mother will love him unconditionally. That belief is born with the child and nurtured until he knows it to be true. With adoptees, the message is one of deception. First you learn that your real mother didn't want you, and then you understand that your adopted parents will love you under the condition that you pretend you are really theirs and act like a child of theirs would act. You are asked to give up any biological traits or pulls and to perform absolutely as requested. Again, let me point out, while this is common, I am speaking of my own situation.

I learned to be a chameleon, to have a sixth sense in knowing what people expected and wanted from me. This is the Artificial Self I mentioned. "Me" didn't exist; the chameleon did. I often questioned my existence. A misty haze surrounded whatever life experience I was participating in. It was an unreality, as if my life was something borrowed, to be returned later.

The Forbidden Self eventually shows itself, usually around puberty. The frustration, the sadness and anger about being cut off from our biological selves sets in. When it becomes evident that we carry genetic traits that don't match our adoptive parents, trouble begins. We can't pretend anymore. We recognize we don't fit and don't belong. Usually, this Forbidden Self is secret, hidden. It's where the adopted child discovers the time tunnel that can transport him or her to a place to fantasize about his or her "roots."

Many do as I did and set out on a journey to find themselves, dodging dangers and falling into other ways of life. The source of the pain is unrelenting, a life of genealogical bewilderment. I studied faces for years. I watched on subways, in classes, on the streets, for any sign of recognition, in hopes that I'd find my family. I tried for years to find the place where I fit in.

Everyone experiences parts of this journey. It's part of the developmental process. With adoptees, the beginning isn't there, so nothing else makes sense. They are born with a part totally erased, with no foundation to stand on, no place to start.

As I sat in the field after the memorial, I knew I was home. There was a cellular recognition that home had been there all along. Dali was, in fact, the symbol for my birth mother. All those years of searching for Dali were in reality my search for my mother, the woman who gave birth to me. Yet here I was, alone in the field with *this field's* Dali, and still I didn't fit. What did that mean? What would come next? Was this the end?

I never got to know my mother the way a daughter should know her mother. I never got to experience that much-needed mothering. How does one move on from that? Within a short time after her death, a tsunami of emotional chaos emerged. All of the unleashed emotions crashed through my defenses. I was overcome by paralyzing grief, and recognizing the loss of what could have been, shattered my psyche. I was left physically and emotionally drained and barely functioning, not knowing what to do or who I was. I did the only thing my body and mind would allow: I went into seclusion to try and put the pieces back together.

It was terrifying to be alone and to sit with those emotions and be soaked by the tears of five decades of loss. I was in a depth of grief no wall could contain. I had found my mother and lost her all in the same breath of never knowing each other. The years of repressed tears came as oceans, with tides I could not control.

The Jungian analyst Clarrisa Pinkola Estes says this about tears: "They can create a river around the boat that carries your soul-life. Tears lift your boat off the rocks, off dry ground, carrying it downriver to someplace new, someplace better." I clung to her words like a lifeline.

What I didn't know at the time was that this shattering and fragmentation is normal in reunion situations. Emotions become overwhelming at some point, and the only choice is to withdraw. I needed silence and solace to put my fragmented self back together again, but in a different order. I began writing and slowly transforming my pain into words on paper. Life became a spiritual death and rebirth of the whole person I am now.

Part of my need to withdraw was physical. My body had taken over and demanded rest. I discovered I had been battling a rare mast cell disease most of my life. Each trauma in my life had bumped up the disease a notch, and finally, all those strange times of illness made sense. The stress of the reunion had sent my mast cells over the edge. Genetic discoveries enabled me to put the pieces of the medical puzzle together. Finally, the mystery was solved. The rights to updated medical history should be accessible to adoptees. Sometimes it's too late.

Several years later, I discovered our birth father. Having written *Finding Heart Horse* and *The Wall of Secrets*, I continue on my journey, excited to see what's just around the corner.

I carry Dali, along with Heart Horse, knowing now that I do exist. I am one self, my true self, still with many cracks to "let the light in," as Leonard Cohen so eloquently sings.

The journey itself is the beginning of the healing. Like peeling an onion, you peel back the layers until you reach the core, and then you dig some more and find the diamonds that were there all along. My spiritual practice gave me the strength to dig that deep.

My secrets, my story, now live in my words inside the covers of *Finding Heart Horse* and *The Wall of Secrets.*

Whatever you face, adopted or not, if you believe you will survive and thrive, then you will. Our thoughts are powerful beyond belief.

We can choose our paths. I hope between the covers of *Finding Heart Horse* and *The Wall of Secrets*, you find inspiration and hope.

Buddhists say that pain is inevitable, but suffering is not. Learn to let go of the causes of your suffering. Whether they be thoughts, emotions, desires, toxic people, negativity, whatever is making you unhappy, let it go. Find within *yourself* the happiness you are looking for in other places.

It's there, I promise you.

You had it all along.

May beings have happiness and the causes of happiness;
May all be free from sorrow and the causes of sorrow;
May all never be separated from the sacred
happiness, which is sorrow-less;
And may all live in equanimity, without too
much attachment and too much aversion;
And live believing in the equality of all that live.
—Traditional Buddhist Prayer

Recommended Reading

Follette, Victoria, PhD, and Jacqueline Pistorello, PhD
Finding Life Beyond Trauma
Guilford Press, 2007

Lifton, Betty Jean
Journey of the Adopted Self: A Quest for Wholeness
Basic Books, 1994
Lost and Found: The Adoption Experience
Harper & Row, 1988

Verrier, Nancy
The Primal Wound: Understanding the Adopted Child
Gateway Press, Inc., 2007
Coming Home to Self: The Adopted Child Grows Up
Gateway Press, Inc., 2003

Brodzinsky, David, and Schecter, Marshal with Marantz, Henig
Being Adopted: The Lifelong Search for Self
Anchor Press, 1998

Trinder, Elizabeth
The Adoption Reunion Handbook
Wiley and Sons, Ltd, 2004

Epstein, Mark
The Trauma of Everyday Life
Penguin Press, 2013

CPSIA information can be obtained at www.ICGtesting.com
Printed in the USA
LVOW07s2342230215

428028LV00004B/42/P